Miss

Dinah
Shore

A Biography

Michael B. Druxman

Miss

Dinah
Shore

A Biography

Michael B. Druxman

BearManor
Media

Albany, Georgia

Published in the USA by
BearManor Media
P.O. Box 71426
Albany, GA 31708
www.BearManorMedia.com

ISBN: 1-59393-847-0

Printed in the United States of America

For my wonderful wife,
Sandy

Table of Contents

Acknowledgments

MISS DINAH SHORE IS AN UNAUTHORIZED BIOGRAPHY. THROUGH THEIR respective representatives in the late 1970s, I approached Miss Shore and her former husband, George Montgomery, for interviews; however, both declined to become involved in this project. Their refusal to cooperate also made it difficult for me to obtain direct testimony from a number of other important people in their lives, including Ticker Freeman, Henry Jaffe, Elizabeth Shore Seligman, Burt Reynolds, and a few more. All quotes in this volume attributed to Dinah and these others were extracted from various magazine and newspaper stories. I also conducted my own interviews in Los Angeles, New York and Tennessee.

In researching this biography, I was fortunate to meet numerous other close friends, relatives and associates of Dinah Shore who collectively knew her well – as far back as her childhood days in Winchester, Tennessee, right up through the end of her life. They were gracious and candid in their remarks, and for this I hereby express my gratitude.

Able researchers throughout the country have supplied me with virtually every important piece of printed material on my subject that has appeared over the years and, in this regard, I would like to thank the original interviewers/ writers of these pieces who, in most cases, asked the right questions so that my job was easier.

The vast majority of this biography was actually written in the late 1970s, but due to a legal dispute between the original paperback and hardback publishers, it was prevented from seeing print at that time. The manuscript lay virtually forgotten in my storage space until recently when I re-discovered, reactivated and updated it.

As they say: Better late than never.

Prologue

It's ten fifty-one when the Western Airlines jet touches down at Las Vegas' McCarran Field. Howard Keel, with his bearded press agent behind him, is the first to disembark the plane, walking quickly up the ramp, on through the airport terminal, then downstairs to the cab stand on the street level

"Where to?" the driver asks, as he takes the actor-singer's suit bag.

"The MGM Grand."

"Silly question," muses the cabbie, belatedly recognizing his passenger.

Though in his fifties, the tall, rugged baritone star of such Metro musical hits as *Seven Brides for Seven Brothers* and *Show Boat* has aged relatively little since he romanced leading ladies like Kathryn Grayson and Esther Williams. True, his thick hair is graying and a few lines lightly etch his face, but these features, as well as his full mustache, serve to make the star even more handsome than in his years at the Culver City studio.

Keel is in town on this morning in 1975 to tape a segment of Dinah Shore's award-winning variety-talk show. Usually, "Dinah!" originates from CBS Television City at Beverly and Fairfax in Los Angeles, but this week five of her ninety-minute afternoon programs are being pre-recorded in the sweltering Nevada fun spot.

"How long has it been since you worked with Dinah?" asks the publicist as they're being chauffeured to the Strip.

"Quite awhile," replies Keel, trying to recall. "We were on a Buick special together back in New York and I also did one of the 'Chevy Shows.' They had me sing 'You'll Never Walk Alone' on that one."

From his tone, the publicist gathers that Howard is not too fond of the Rodgers and Hammerstein piece.

The Grand, like so much of the celluloid product that was churned out by MGM during Hollywood's "Golden Era," is ornately huge – a hulking sterile structure that has been built with the idea of making even Vegas' most lavish hotels look like the Holiday Inns by comparison. It succeeds – almost too well.

Upon entering the lobby, which overlooks what is probably the largest casino in town, Keel and his friend are directed to the Ziegfeld Room, the home of the hotel's fabulous nighttime revue, *Hallelujah, Hollywood*, but now serving as the television studio for "Dinah!" Every day this week, the program tapes on the oversized stage between two and three-thirty, then the auditorium is turned back to the hotel staff to be prepared for the eight-thirty dinner crowd.

Doing a television show away from the totally controlled atmosphere of a studio has its problems. The program's talk segments must be kept to a minimum, since there are no viewing monitors in the audience, and the production staff and technicians find that it's not always easy to fit their cumbersome equipment into a facility not built to accommodate it. On the other hand, by originating from the Ziegfeld Room, the show can make use of the well-designed sets from *Hallelujah, Hollywood* and in fact, play before a different one every day.

On this particular segment, the opulent Persian décor of the *Kismet* set is being employed as backdrop, which makes it logical for the show's talent coordinators to have booked Howard Keel – the star of the 1955 movie version of *Kismet* – as the principal guest. Lovely Lola Falana, who is currently headlining in the hotel's Celebrity Theater; stammering country-western artist Mel Tillis; and funnyman Ronnie Schell, will join him. They're expensive talent, but for this and other shows of the genre, performers sell their services for AFTRA (American Federation of Television and Radio Artists) scale of $371.75.

More important than the cash is the fact that by doing talkers with Dinah, Merv Griffin, Johnny Carson, Mike Douglas, or the like, the star is afforded the invaluable opportunity of plugging to millions of viewers whatever he currently has going in his career, be it a movie, a television special, a record album, or a book. Indeed, it's claimed by some that a talk host need only *show* a new book *once* on national television and sales for that volume will double.

Entertainers who earn a good deal of their income from either nightclubs or regional dinner theaters benefit greatly from exposure on these shows. Many of them swear there is a direct correlation between the number of such appearances they make each year and their frequency of in-person bookings.

Keel and his rep stride into the Ziegfeld Room to find dozens of technicians and program personnel scurrying about in preparation for the afternoon's taping. Down in front of the stage, Dinah, attired in a chic blue denim casual suit with red-checked blouse, is discussing one of her numbers with musical director John Rodby.

For a lady in her early sixties, this five-foot six, 123-pound star with honey blonde hair looks sensational. It is truly difficult to conceive of her being any older than forty.

Spotting Keel, she interrupts her conference and goes over to her guest, greeting him warmly, not as a casual show business acquaintance, but as she would an old friend who has been invited to her home. The baritone will discover later from production staff members that Dinah was genuinely thrilled when she learned he would be appearing on the show and even recalled the fact that he is a bass baritone, rather than a lyric baritone (an "insignificant" detail to anyone but a singer and his conductor).

They chat. She asks about his cute year-old daughter and about how things are with him in general, and then she tells of the fun she had recently guesting on an episode of Norman Lear's syndicated soap opera spoof, "Mary Hartman, Mary Hartman."

A few moments pass and Dinah is recalled to her rehearsal while an assistant stage manager shows Howard to a makeshift dressing room. Located upstairs above the hotel's kitchen, the quarters are actually utilized evenings by comic David Brenner, who is appearing with Miss Falana on the

MGM nitery bill. Several soiled Kleenex are on the dressing table, making it apparent that the janitor has not yet been through today.

Noon. Keel is back down in the showroom to rehearse the number he will do on the air. It's a medley of songs ("Oh, What a Beautiful Morning," "Make Believe," and "Bless Yore Beautiful Hide") with which he has become identified with over the years and which he uses in his nightclub act. In addition, the producers have asked him to introduce the *Kismet* set by singing "Stranger in Paradise" a number actually sung by Vic Damone in the movie.

The harried staff – especially the ladies – forget their duties for a few minutes and listen to the baritone's resonant voice as he sings the numbers everyone remembers so fondly. After each of his two run-throughs, he receives a hearty round of applause – a tribute that these seasoned professionals bestow on only the very best. Keel is quite pleased with the reaction.

Following a bite to eat in the local hotel's deli-coffee shop (one of the few spots at the MGM that features a décor of movie memorabilia), Howard returns to the Ziegfeld Room for a conference with one of the show's interviewers regarding what he and Dinah will discuss on the program. The writer is interested in the fact that Keel has taken up the guitar these past few years, and they agree that at some point in the show he will borrow Mel Tillis' instrument and perform an impromptu number. Unlike the other talk programs, everything that happens on "Dinah!" is planned as exactly as possible.

The audience has been lining up outside the showroom for over ninety minutes. They are ushered to their tables shortly after one-thirty. Many of the casually dressed tourists have never seen a movie star in person – let alone been to a television show taping – and despite the entertaining warm-up provided by announcer Johnny Gilbert, they impatiently await the main event to begin.

Upstairs, the cramped green room, complete with bar and bartender begins to hum with activity as production staff members, the show's guests, and their various agents, personal managers, and publicists crowd in to watch the program on a closed-circuit monitor. Keel, having changed into his custom-tailored work clothes, talks a bit with Mel Tillis and Ronnie Schell, then, since he is to be the first guest, is whisked away by an assistant director to join Dinah backstage.

It's show time. The seventeen-piece orchestra plays the opening bars of the star's familiar theme song, "Dinah," from which she adopted her professional name so long ago. Johnny Gilbert announces, "Ladies and gentlemen, Miss Dinah Shore." and the lady steps into the spotlight, waiting for the audience's enthusiastic applause to die before she sings the melodic "It's All Right With Me." (In the green room, her arranger, Norman Martin, listens intently to her phrasing of the tune.)

More applause. Dinah gives her usual "down home" welcome to her appreciative audience, then there's a commercial break before she returns to introduce "that handsome star of MGM musicals...Howard Keel."

He makes his entrance from the top of a high staircase, moving down to center stage as he delights the crowd with his medley. The response is tremendous and, following another commercial, he joins the hostess for a chat on a large Persian throne, situated stage left.

Lola Falana is up next to sing a tune from her act. Later, when she makes the grouping on the throne a threesome – with Keel between the lovely ladies and obviously enjoying every minute of it – the informal and witty chatter is more like that of a party, rather than a talk show. Of course, the real wine they're sipping certainly helps to create this relaxed atmosphere.

"They sure as hell are having a good time," chuckles someone upstairs. Perhaps it's because this is Las Vegas, but the tension that usually fills the green room back home at the studio is absent today. The hard-to-impress pros are also having fun.

An often-seen performer on "Dinah!" is Mel Tillis, who today warbles his new single, "Love Revival," then talks with the hostess away from the previously introduced guests. Before they rejoin the others, Dinah takes center stage again to sing her second number of the day, "The Hungry Years."

Ronnie Schell has also done the show a lot, but this is the first time he has been asked to perform a stand-up routine. Since the program is originating from Vegas, the producers wanted to book a comic who plays the local nightspots, and as Ron is a particular favorite of Dinah's ("I'm a health food nut and for a while I'd come on the show and mix her health food cocktails."), he's been chosen for the assignment. His original material and deft technique goes over extremely well with the audience – both upstairs and out front.

"You know," he tells Dinah as he joins her and the other guests in the semi-circle of chairs that are so common to talkers, "this is the first time

I've ever been in Las Vegas and not been booked into a club. It feels kind of funny."

Everybody's on now. For the twenty minutes remaining, it's one big seemingly off-the-cuff, gab session. Lola relates an embarrassing experience that happened to her once on the Johnny Carson show; Keel strums on Mel Tillis' guitar; and the country artist mentions that he's recently changed his record company affiliation – from *MGM* to *MCA*. Hospitably, Dinah does anything but dominate the conversation, speaking up only to encourage one of the celebrities to enlarge on a previous statement or to draw out an anecdote the production staff has come across in their pre-show probings.

There's a final cutaway for advertisers, then Miss Shore has only a few seconds to thank her guests for appearing with her and to quickly plug their latest endeavors. Music. Applause. Another ninety-minute program is in the can.

"Good show!" announces a staff member, leaving the green room to start her clean-up chores for today's entry. The talent representatives also head down the long undecorated hallway toward the freight elevator, which will bring their individual clients up from the kitchen area to their dressing rooms.

It is at this moment – after the program has concluded – that one can see the difference between the way guests feel about "Dinah!" and the other expertly-produced and moderated talk programs on which many of them appear. With Merv, Johnny, and the rest, a personality can have an enjoyable time with the affable host, but they're ever conscious that they're on to be interviewed and to entertain. Afterwards, it seems as if each tries to be the first one out the stage door. Not that they have any place in particular to go, but there's no good reason to stick around.

Merv, for example, believes – and perhaps rightly so – that he'll achieve a more extemporaneous discussion if he doesn't mix with his guests before or after the program. On the air, he forms questions based on notes compiled from staff-conducted interviews. The celebrities understand his philosophy and aren't offended at his not socializing with them following the evening's wrap.

Conversely, Dinah doesn't try to catch her guests off-guard. While her staff also does in-depth interviews with each personality before the show, the guests are informed of the particular anecdotes the hostess will expect them to relate or of any special stunt or demonstration in which they'll be asked to participate. Seldom does Dinah depart from her planned scenario. The resulting show may seem rather choreographed, but guests are usually more relaxed and develop more camaraderie than they do on other talk shows; thus, people tend to linger awhile after "Dinah!" is over. In the hallway outside the dressing rooms, the hostess, Keel, and Miss Falana stop to visit – continuing the conversation that was cut short on the show. Nobody, it seems, really wants to say goodbye.

A few minutes later, while Howard is changing into his street clothes and his publicist is on the phone confirming plane reservations back to Los Angeles, Mel Tillis and his manager stop by the dressing room to talk. The adieu lasts over twenty minutes, with the two singers sitting down and reminiscing about mutual friends in Nashville.

Three quarters of an hour after the taping has ended, Keel and his representative are downstairs in front of the hotel, signaling a taxi. Their rearranged flight is to depart McCarran in thirty minutes, so they're in a bit of a rush. As the vehicle pulls up, the publicist comments to his client: "It was an entertaining show. I think you'll be very happy when you see it."

"It felt good," Keel replies, getting into the cab. "I'd forgotten how much fun it is to work with Dinah. She really makes you feel at home." The star instructs the driver and it's only a matter of moments before the cab is zooming down the Strip toward the airport.

***

For over five decades, Dinah Shore made her audiences and co-workers "feel at home." She had that rare ability to induce a state of happy well-being into people wherever she appeared, resulting in a continued love affair between her and her followers. It was nearly impossible for one to watch Dinah perform or to meet her in person and not come away from the experience liking this fine, gracious lady who loved people and practiced living life to the fullest.

In the fickle world of popular music, where artists rise with rocket-like speed to fame and fortune, only to fall from grace just as quickly, Dinah had a longer and more steady run at the top than any other girl singer. She far outlasted the incomparable Kate Smith; managed to maintain a brighter star than such talented – and at times *hotter* – contemporaries as Patti Page, Jo Stafford, and Rosemary Clooney; and though some may argue to the contrary, she kept pace in popularity with movie queen Doris Day, whom she preceded in the business by several years. Indeed, if a poll were taken to choose the most popular male and female vocalists of the past seventy years, the probable winners would be either Frank Sinatra or Elvis Presley for the men and, for the ladies, Dinah Shore.

When it came to "the tube," Dinah had no equal in the musical field. And were it not for a zany redhead named Lucille Ball, with whom Dinah must vie for the honor, she could easily be dubbed "the first lady of television." Dinah endured primarily because of her ability to adapt her talents to the ever-changing tastes of her public. From her forties hits like "Yes, My Darling Daughter," "Blues in the Night," and "The Anniversary Song," to some of her later country recordings, the versatile lady never allowed herself to become entrenched within a single musical fashion. "That may be the only reason I've survived," she once admitted. "I certainly haven't had many big sellers. I've always tried to stay current."

The winner of almost every major honor in her profession, including trade publication polls, the coveted Emmy and Peabody television awards and even the Gallup Poll naming her one of the most-admired women in the world, Dinah adjusted not only her musical abilities in a successful effort to stay on top, but also her public image. As good friend, comic Dick Martin, once explained: "Dinah has lasted because, unlike so many ladies in this business, she can *talk*. She's an interesting, well-read person who is good company. Today, her singing is secondary. It's incidental. People think of her as a hostess…a *personality* and, as such, she'll be on top for as long as she wants to be."

Dinah's personal life over the years was anything but placid, yet friends and fellow workers swear that she never allowed her problems to affect her relationships with others. No matter what might be bothering her, she was invariably warm and friendly with whomever she came in contact, choosing to keep her personal troubles private.

"She's not real," quipped one Hollywood comedian. "It's like God had some clay left over and said, 'What'll I do with it? I know. I'll make a Dinah Shore.'"

The late, great pianist-wit Oscar Levant once announced that his doctor ordered him not to watch Dinah because of his diabetes. Later, he expressed the wish that she would take sadness lessons.

On a more serious level, Henry Jaffe, producer of "Dinah," once commented: "There's a wall around her that nobody penetrates. She never shows her real feelings in public. She's easily hurt and terribly sensitive. She wants more than anything else to be loved, and I don't think I've ever seen her really show anger. I'm sorry about that. She'd probably be better off if she could blow off some steam."

As for Dinah, she described her "formula for living" as being able to "forget everything that happened yesterday and live in the present."

Perhaps it was the hurts and obstacles she had to deal with during her lifetime that gave this southern-born gentlewoman such an exceptional ability to maintain her wholesome charm and dignity in the most trying circumstances. Her early years, for example, were not ones that would nurture emotional security in any child.

The victim of polio by the time she was two, Dinah – with the help of her strong-willed mother – overcame her physical disability. But the affliction and the fact that she was not then particularly attractive and was a Jewish girl in a predominantly Christian community created strong self-doubts, which may have been instrumental in driving her to excel in whatever she attempted.

A less than peaceful relationship between her parents also affected her. "I always felt I shouldn't express disagreement or anger," she once said. "It was impolite. Shouting was rude. My mother shouted at my father. I made a pact when I was a little girl: I would never shout or disagree with my man. On my talk show, I'll never humiliate a guest. But I will disagree. I won't make it a word contest, but I will express my opinion."

When Dinah was in her teens, her mother died, and her older sister and brother-in-law guided her into adulthood. After graduating from Vanderbilt University, she left Nashville – against her prosaic father's wishes – to seek fame and fortune as a singer in New York. That first year in the Big Town was a lean one. There were times, in fact, when she wanted to return to Tennessee, but she was persistent.

It wasn't too many years – once she'd come to the attention of comedian Eddie Cantor – before she was voted the country's favorite female recording artist, eventually garnering a total of nineteen gold records. She had also married the man of her dreams, tall, handsome romantic actor George Montgomery. For almost eighteen years, as far as the outside world was concerned, that marriage was one of the happiest in Hollywood. At the same time, Dinah was becoming one of television's most beloved stars.

December of 1961 was the month in which Dinah Shore Montgomery's "blissful" private life was smashed, for it was then that the vocalist separated from her husband. There had been trouble brewing for quite awhile, but ever the lady, Dinah had kept these personal problems from the attention of even her closest associates.

Despite some unpleasant rumors, the marriage ended with dignity – neither partner rebuking the other publicly. It was only in later years that Dinah, perhaps owing to her early-bred insecurities, expressed openly her doubts about the basic relationship: "I never knew in my heart of hearts if he had picked me because of me, or because I was Dinah Shore. If I had remained Fanny Rose Shore (her real name) – then what? Would George have loved me? Would he have wanted *me*?"

Soon after the divorce, Dinah drastically cut her professional activities to occasional club dates and television specials in order to devote more time to her children. She married again, but in this instance the union was a total mistake. The resulting dissolution created a number of lurid, if untrue, newspaper headlines suggesting that the songstress had been involved in a number of extramarital affairs.

Things went relatively smoothly for Dinah after she returned to full-time television action in 1970. Hostessing her daily afternoon variety-talk show – first on NBC, then on CBS and finally independently syndicated out of Los Angeles – gave her the opportunity to say goodbye to nightclub audiences, to just be herself and express her ideas in a relaxing, home-like setting. When some critics harped at the plushness of "Dinah's Place," (her NBC talker), the lady retorted: "Who the hell cares if you live under conditions like this or you live in a rent-controlled apartment? The problems are the same. Yes, I live in a glamorous way. I don't deny it. I am not ashamed of it. I earned it. I worked for it. But my problems aren't different from other women: children, work, ecology – yes, it's been discussed *ad nauseam*, but there's more to say and we'll say it – consumer fraud, how to attract a man…"

Attracting a man was never really a problem with Dinah. Once, in fact, she was the envy of most women, having been involved in a well-publicized relationship with screen sex symbol and *Cosmopolitan* model, Burt Reynolds.

This, then, is the basis of Dinah's story, from her turbulent childhood, through her career struggles and troubled marriages, to the secure pinnacle of success, which she retained for over five decades. It's a saga that touches nearly the entire spectrum of show business, and involves many legendary stars. Yet, of greatest importance, it's a tale of how love and strength of character merged to give us one of the world's most exceptional women.

1.

The Tennessee Years

WHEN SOLOMON AARON SHORE EMIGRATED TO THE UNITED STATES FROM Russia in the early part of the last century, he was seeking a better life, one rich with opportunities for every man, regardless of his religion. Anti-Semitic feelings were rampant in the old country under the Czar, and the fact that Shore – born about 1879 – was the grandson of a rabbi, made conditions worse for him.

Like so many travelers who made similar journies, Solomon had heard stories of the new nation on the other side of the Atlantic Ocean that offered good fortune to anyone who had the initiative. Being a pragmatist, he realized that the tales of easy riches and streets paved with gold were fantasy, but at the very least, maybe hard work in America might bring a just reward. Anything was better than the oppression he endured in Eastern Europe.

His family, most of whom were religious teachers and leaders, objected to his proposed move. They wanted him to remain with them and to follow in the traditions of his ancestors. But Solomon's mind was made up. Despite the protests of his loved ones, he departed on the arduous trip, which took him many weeks to complete.

Once in the United States, Solomon Shore prospered and built himself a financial stake to start his own business. He also married. The lady was Anna Stein, who was twelve years his junior. Anna Stein was also a Russian immigrant. She'd been born in Kiev and brought to this country as a young girl by her older sister, Lena.

Lena had been the first of the Stein family – which included four sisters and a brother – to come to America. And after marrying Samuel Bittner, who operated a costume rental business, she sent for her siblings, one at a time. Anna was the first to follow. Her sister and brother-in-law welcomed her into their home in Nashville, Tennessee, where she learned English, grew into womanhood, and eventually met and married Solomon Shore.

Solomon and Anna were an unusual-looking couple. "She was a large-framed woman," recalls a former neighbor, "and he was somewhat smaller. Both spoke with accents, but his was much thicker than hers."

The Shores left Nashville and traveled through Tennessee's lush green countryside to Winchester, the Franklin County Seat, with a population of about twenty-five hundred, located in the Cumberland Valley near the Alabama border. Their plan was to open a small dry goods store. When they arrived, Solomon and Anna went to the local bank, where they opened an account and also spoke to the manager of their plan. "I wouldn't advise your doing that, Mr. Shore," said the seemingly sympathetic banker. "You'll lose all your savings."

"I don't understand," replied Solomon.

"Winchester is a small place, and unfortunately, you can't do anything much about people's prejudices. The last Jewish storekeeper we had didn't last six months."

"But I plan to *stay*," Shore told the man quietly.

It wasn't easy being the only Jewish couple in a town that had many residents belonging to the Ku Klux Klan, yet Solomon was determined. He'd already fled once from persecution, and perhaps now he felt it was time he stopped running and faced the problem head-on. Anna, too, was for standing firm.

Like so many Southern and Midwestern towns, Winchester has its business district built around the county courthouse. The Shores located their store just off this main square. Solomon was both resented and an object of curiosity for a time, but the store did well. "I built it up by hard work and fair dealings," he would say in later years. Indeed, it wasn't very long before he had established branches in the nearby town of Decherd and Manchester.

Proud of their cultural background, and wishing to prove they could be first-rate citizens, the Shores became active in Winchester's cultural and civic affairs. Within a few years, both had earned the respect and acceptance of their neighbors. Solomon attained the position of Junior Deacon in the Masons; Anna, dubbed "Shorey" by her friends, rose to Grand Matron of the Eastern Star, and later was elected president of the PTA.

Solomon and Anna had two children – both daughters. Elizabeth, or "Bessie," was the first to come along, and eight years later, on February 29, 1916, Frances "Fanny" Rose Shore was born. (Though Dinah's formal biographies claim she was born on March 1, 1917, old Tennessee newspaper accounts and her friends back in Nashville and Winchester insist she was a Leap Year baby. Leap Year was 1916.)

Although Elizabeth was subjected to cruel anti-Semitic taunts from her playmates, by the time "Fanny" was old enough to be aware of prejudice, much of it had dissipated. True, there was always some strangeness in people's manner toward her, but with Jews comprising less than one percent of the primarily Protestant state's population, this was understandable. After all, what did a United Methodist or Southern Baptist know of Rosh Hashana or Yom Kippur? And it must have seemed odd to see the Sabbath observed on Saturday rather than Sunday.

Fanny, despite the generally cordial treatment she received from the townspeople, did not altogether escape the uglier aspects of life in a small Southern community. The Ku Klux Klan – that "noble" brotherhood of white bigots – had been founded in Pulaski, Tennessee in 1886, so it wasn't unusual to see a group of the white-hooded hooligans marching down the streets of most communities – particularly those in rural sections of the State.

Young Fanny watched such a demonstration with her father in Winchester. As the disturbing parade passed by them, Solomon named every man in the group, many of them supposedly friends and neighbors. He'd identified each by his shoes or the way he walked, and as his daughter recalled in a 1972

3

interview with *Good Housekeeping*, he was quite upset by the incident: "He never had violent emotions, and I couldn't get over his anger that night. I've never forgotten it."

The Shores lived in a small wood frame house at 308 2nd Avenue, where Fanny Rose played with another child named Elizabeth Cheshire, (Mrs. O. D. Miller): "We used to play dolls and croquet together. I remember that Dinah was scared to death of ghosts. She wouldn't go near dark places, nor would she go higher than the third step of my house; she was sure the ghosts would get her if she went up there. At night, neither of us would walk home alone, even though we just lived two doors apart. Dinah's older sister, Bessie, had to walk with us."

When another neighbor, W. D. Krauth, bought the first radio in Winchester, Fanny and Elizabeth would visit him regularly, taking turns using the earphones.

If Fanny developed any feeling of defensiveness over being Jewish, she more than likely absorbed it from her high-spirited, gregarious mother. Anna always seemed to be trying to prove her quality – a trait that caused conflict both in the Shore household and at the store where she worked parttime. She was a natural athlete who excelled in everything she attempted: golf, tennis, swimming, and dancing. She possessed a rich mezzo-soprano voice and there was a time when she secretly took voice lessons in a neighboring town, hoping to sing in an operetta. Her non-artistic husband, though proud of his lovely young wife's accomplishments, ordered them stopped. His hard-earned money was not going to be wasted on something as frivolous as singing lessons.

Shy and quiet by nature, Solomon was a practical man, interested in little more than business. His early experiences had taught him that money should be saved for a rainy day. But for Anna, "the future" was too far away. She wanted to spend money, because she felt that life should be enjoyed today. These differing attitudes about finances, as well as the couple's wide age difference and nearly complete lack of similar tastes, combined to form an atmosphere of almost constant turbulence in which Bessie and Fanny grew up. As Dinah once remarked, "Mother and Daddy's different personalities pulled us one way and then another like a tug of war."

Though Solomon earned a comfortable living for his family, the Shores were by no means wealthy. "We were just average people," recalled Dinah, "with one good silver services and one special set of linen. We were like so many average Americans."

Francis Rose was just over eighteen months old when she came down with a strange fever that left her right leg semi-paralyzed and that local doctors had trouble diagnosing. Her father took her to New York to see several specialists. Their diagnosis: poliomyelitis.

When she heard the terrible news, Anna was torn between pity and frustration of her ambitions for her child. She had been unable to pursue a singing career, and had hoped that her daughter might fulfill this dream for her. But now that didn't seem very likely. She, Solomon, and a black nurse named Alice Trigg religiously followed the doctor's prescription of therapeutic – and painful – leg massage and manipulation. The therapy was developed by Sister Kenny and was continued until Dinah was fourteen. Anna refused to acknowledge that Dinah even had polio – possibly to prevent her child from sensing her concern, or perhaps it was a misguided attempt to be considerate. But her seemingly harsh attitude caused Fanny deep feelings of inferiority. Dinah later commented: "I know that she had tenderness and love for me, but I wasn't sure then."

There was, for example, that day when Anna took her lame little girl out to the park so she could ride her tricycle. Fanny clambered onto the vehicle, grasping tight to the handlebars, and slowly pressed the pedal with her weakened right foot. The trike moved, but only at a snail's pace.

"Come on," snapped Anna, watching Dinah from a nearby bench. "Pedal up. Your foot's all right." A couple of other little children noticed Fanny and began to tease her. "Come on, pedal up!" her mother shouted as the girl pushed forward, trying not to cry.

Awhile later, she overheard her mother's challenging comment, "I suppose she'll have to learn to walk all over again."

"I felt disgraced," Dinah later reflected. "I thought the rest of the kids shied away from me for fear they'd catch a dreadful disease. I tried to cover up, but underneath I was painfully self-conscious about it until I was grown, and never told anyone who didn't already know. With those who did, I desperately tried to prove I wasn't different or handicapped. And, at home, my affliction was a forbidden word."

Her classmates at Winchester Grammar School taunted the chronically underweight, limping and unattractive Miss Shore, which didn't make her life any easier: "Fanny Rose sat on a tack. Did Fanny rise? Shore!"

Dinah: "I tell you, it just made me go home nights and chew my pillow."

Although Dinah suffered most at the hands of children, ironically it was a child who helped her put her problem into true perspective. On another occasion, Fanny, all bundled up for the winter weather, was playing hopscotch outside her house with neighbor children and, without really being aware of it, began favoring her right foot. "Francis!" yelled her mother from the front door. "What have I always told you about that foot? What do you think your friends will think of you? You ought to be ashamed!"

Fanny made no reply. Embarrassed, she merely looked at her friends helplessly and then down at the ground, wishing all along she wasn't there. When Anna had returned to her household chores, Dinah turned to her companions and said, "You must hate me. Maybe I should go home."

"Don't be stupid," said one of the children. "My mother's always bawling me out about something."

This was a meaningful incident in Dinah's life, as she told interviewers in the late fifties: "I often think of that day now because I learned something very important. It was that as long as you dislike or are afraid of accepting yourself as you really are, people won't be ready to accept or like you. You don't have to be perfect for people to like you...you just have to be yourself.

"And I also know *now* that my mother's refusal to be very sympathetic with me and her insistence that I join in sports which involved a great deal of exercise, was not because she was ashamed of my handicap but because she was determined that I shouldn't find a psychological crutch to lean on.

"There were relentless dancing lessons, swimming, and ballet, and in each I had to prove myself to the hilt. This absolute drive to compete physically gave me the drive to compete on every level. I never wanted sympathy; I just didn't want to be considered different."

Suffering from a desperate need to feel loved, Dinah attempted to develop abilities that she thought her mother and usually undemonstrative father would admire, but as might be expected, she pushed too hard, becoming, in her words, "a pretty objectionable showoff."

Before she could even talk well, she was standing on a counter and entertaining the more patient customers in her father's department store by singing, "Here I stand with two little chips. Who will kiss my pretty lips?" Though he pretended to disapprove of her antics, Solomon actually got a kick out of them and, on occasion, would block the way of customers trying to exit during a performance.

Alice Trigg recalled: "Dinah's voice was always loud. Once I heard it clear up to the courthouse."

"When she was eight," mused sister Bessie, "she'd beg to come into the parlor and play her ukulele and sing for my boyfriends. It was a mistake to let her. She never knew when to quit."

A couple of years later, when Frances Rose was regularly hamming it up at her mother's Ladies Aid group, at PTA meetings and at school, she decided to impress her classmates by glamorizing her nickname. She added a final "e", making it "Fannye."

"I was pretty unlovable," said Dinah.

Anna put her daughter in her proper place after one of her overdone exhibitions. Driving home from what Fanny considered to be a triumphant performance in a school play, the girl asked how she did. "I don't think you were very polite," answered her mother.

Caught offguard, Frances asked what Anna meant.

"Be considerate of other people around you. Be a listener, as well as an actor, if you want to be liked."

It was good advice, which Dinah followed successfully throughout her long career.

When Fanny was about eight, Solomon sold his S.A. Shore Department Stores to Abe Sanders, a relative, and moved his family to Nashville, which at the time was boasting a population of 120,000. The move was made for the benefit of the two girls. Both Anna and Solomon agreed that their daughters would receive a better education in the Tennessee state capital and would also have the opportunity to socialize with other Jewish youngsters. They purchased a red brick duplex at 3745 Whitland Avenue, and rented out half of it. Quiet and lined with maple trees, Whitland Avenue was in one of Nashville's finer sections, and it was close to the Shore's synagogue, the Vine Street Temple.

In Nashville, Solomon Shore had various business and real estate interests, but according to one family member, "he'd already made his money in Winchester and was really semi-retired."

"Uncle Solomon was a fine man," recalled Dinah's first cousin, Dodie Bittner (Mrs. Leo Jaffe). "He was quiet and very scholarly. I remember him sitting in his big chair and we kids having to be very quiet around him."

Dodie, the daughter of Lena and Samuel Bittner, was the same age as Dinah. The girls were best of friends. Dinah loved staying overnight at the Bittner residence because the couple were the parents of four daughters.

That singing had always been Frances Rose's first love was no secret to her parents, though she would be in her teens before they would let her study with a professional voice instructor. Nevertheless, still seeking approval, the now more subdued girl would entertain the lifeguards every day at the Cascade Plunge, where she'd go to swim. Strumming her ukulele, she treated the amused guys to half-cocked blues renditions of "My Canary Has Circles Under Its Eyes" and "I Can't Give You Anything But Love, Baby."

What she classified as her first *public* appearance as a singer occurred when she was in the eighth grade when she played her ukulele and sang "Canary" at a school assembly. The performance was less than a smashing success. "Too sophisticated for my audience," she explained.

Like most young girls in the pre or early teens, Frances Rose was stage struck. She and her mother dreamed of her becoming a singer with the Metropolitan Opera. A brief trip to Hollywood with her family when she was a youngster of ten enhanced the idea of fame. Awed by the motion picture capital, she collected autographs from any bus driver who had even *seen* a movie star.

Fanny was only fourteen when she made her "professional" singing debut at a nightclub-gambling house outside of Nashville called The Pines. In order to get a job in the roadhouse – which ordinarily did not allow minors on the premises – she lied about her age to the orchestra leader. Then without telling her folks, she stole home to borrow Bessie's best party dress, a pair of her high-heeled shoes, and some of her make-up: "I made myself look what I thought was glamorous, and got out of the house before anyone could see me."

It was an important night for her and she wanted everything to go just right. She was not only getting her first shot at "big time" show business, but she was also being paid ten dollars per night – money that would buy some new clothes she wanted.

Accompanied by cousin Dodie, who was there to lend moral support, the masquerading teenager arrived at The Pines on schedule, went over her numbers with the orchestra leader, then tried to relax before her first set. Everything seemed to be going as planned. "Under a Blanket of Blue" was her first number and she sang it in a spotlight. It went rather well, despite the fact that she was a little nervous, but when the full stage lights went on, young Frances Rose was shocked. Sitting ringside with two of their friends were Mom and Dad: "Mother blinked. Dad winked. I went on singing, and after the show I ran home as fast as a taxi and my feet could carry me. If I was going to be scolded, I could take it better at home."

Dinah's would-be clandestine debut resulted in the suspension of all social privileges for two weeks. "That was the last nightclub I saw for quite a spell," she reported.

Formal music lessons began for Dinah about the same time she started high school. She studied classical piano with Mary Faulkner Winkler, who had her own studio uptown on Seventh. Actually, Anna made her take the lessons and Fanny hated them, so it's not surprising that she learned only a couple of pieces. She did, however, appear in one class recital at the old Nashville Conservatory of Music, where she played to an audience of parents.

Her voice teacher was John A. Lewis, a respected baritone soloist who performed at various functions around Nashville. Dinah was one of his prize students, and he had her join the choir at the First Presbyterian Church – a move that didn't work out too well for the rest of the vocal group. "Everything had to be revoiced for me," remembered Dinah. "I'd sung solo so intensively at home that I couldn't get the hang of harmony singing. Also, even at that age I was a contralto. I was like a boy who'd become a baritone before his voice changed. I got out of the choir before they threw me out."

With her piping soprano voice having turned traitor and become contralto, there didn't seem to be any future for Frances Rose as a singer of serious music: "I lost interest in my voice about the same time the teachers did."

But considering her age, the voice change and her loss of interest in lessons might easily have been predicted. At fifteen – or even much earlier – a normal healthy American girl's interests usually turn from the more somber aspects of life to such fascinating subjects as boys, so, since Frances Rose was certainly normal, healthy, and American, it was only natural that she would follow suit. Thus, while a student at Hume-Fogg, Nashville's only high school, Dinah went out for the cheerleading squad and at every football game could be heard shouting such chants as "Sis Boom Bah, Rah, Rah, Rah" and so forth. Even if she'd wanted to continue her formal vocal training at this point, it would have been difficult because she was constantly yelling herself hoarse. Or, as Dinah said, "I sounded like a frog."

One of her fellow cheerleaders was Lorraine Regen (Mrs. John Thornton, of Brownsville, Tennessee), who recalled that Dinah was one of the few students at Hume-Fogg who had her own automobile: "I have a vivid memory of Fanny Rose, with raven black hair, driving along in her red Chevrolet convertible with black upholstery and singing to herself all the way." (Dinah got the car near the end of her high school years – a graduation present.)

"As cheerleaders," said Mrs. Thornton, "we were quite good friends and dated many of the same boys – A.L. Moore, Hunk Crockett, John Shapiro, and Rip Blackmer. Actually, we went out more as a *gang* of kids, rather than any pair of us going steady. Back in the thirties, we weren't that quick to get 'pinned,' or whatever they used to call it in the fifties and sixties."

Leonard Kornman, owner of the Oxford Shop in Nashville, dated Fanny occasionally during her high school and college years: "Most of the time we'd either go to a dance or to the Cascade Plunge for a swim. She always wore a white bathing suit to show off her tan. At dances, all the other fellows would cut in on us. Her outgoing personality made her a favorite with the boys. She only had one fault that I recall. She was seldom on time."

Throughout her school years and, indeed, her life, Dinah's preference in men always seemed to run toward the athletic type. She dated many football and basketball players back in Nashville. Later, when she began her professional career, she was usually seen on the arm of one of Hollywood's "he-men."

Nashville's young people also enjoyed swimming in the Cumberland River. Dr. John Shapiro recalled such an occasion: "Fanny Rose, myself, and a couple of other kids from Hume-Fogg were sitting on a river bank when I spotted a snake. I wasn't sure if it was poisonous or not, but why take chances? I killed it. At least, I thought I did.

"I put the snake in a can and Fanny started driving us home. Suddenly, the snake started to move. I got real scared, but Fanny stayed calm and stopped the car so we could kick the thing out. Boy, did I feel foolish."

The popular hangout for teenagers in Nashville was an ice cream parlor called Candyland. After school, Hume-Fogg students would walk the two or three blocks up the hill to the corner establishment, then spend the rest of the day sharing chocolate sodas until it was time to drag themselves home for supper. Fanny's favorite snack was cashew nuts.

Candyland, in the 1970s, had changed very little since it was first built back in the early twenties. The décor of dark cherry-wood paneling and cathedral-style mirrors was still present, as was one employee who had worked there since the days when Fanny Rose was a regular customer: "When school was out, the kids would just pour in here. They'd pile in, six to a booth. It was during the Depression and few had any money. They'd sit around, taking turns on one Coke.

"Dinah was in here all the time. Often, she'd just leave her books behind the counter and go shopping."

Whatever disagreeable personality traits Frances Rose had exhibited as a child had definitely disappeared by the time she reached high school, as did almost all signs of her polio bout. Her fellow students – without exception – remember her as being very warm, friendly, and one of the most popular girls in class. Though with her large hooked nose she wasn't the most attractive student ("All I ever had to do to realize that I was no beauty was to look in the mirror."), she was still elected the "best all-around girl" at Hume-Fogg.

Another of her high school classmates, John Roseberry, reported that Miss Shore never forgot the kids she grew up with, even after she became famous: "Dinah came back to Nashville for a visit in the late forties. I hadn't seen her in years, but she picked me right out of a crowd of two hundred people; said 'How are you, John? How's your family?'"

During her high school years, Fanny seemed to be "in love" every minute. But typically, the boys she didn't care for adored her and the ones she wanted were, for the most part, disinterested. There was, for example, the captain of the football team who, for the purposes of this account, will be referred to as "Bill."

Tall and handsome, Bill was pursued by seemingly every girl in school. He and Frances became well acquainted in a Latin class they took together, and before long he was seeing her home at the end of the day. Later, there were invitations to Candyland for a soda, or to the local movie house. Being a born romantic, the impressionable Miss Shore began to imagine that she and her football hero might be together forever. But, then, her dream was slashed apart. Suddenly Bill wasn't around to walk her home from school anymore and he stopped calling. Frances told herself that he was just too busy with football practice or his studies, but deep in her heart she knew that this was probably not true.

When she heard that a club he belonged to was throwing a luncheon and that members were inviting their mothers and girlfriends, Fanny assumed it would be only a day or two before Bill asked her to accompany him. He didn't. Instead, he took one of the prettiest girls at Hume-Fogg.

To any girl of her age, such an experience would be difficult, but for a girl of Frances' sensitivity, it was twice as traumatic. "It took a long time to get over that," she recalled in a 1960 *Photoplay* interview. "I was hurt, terribly hurt, and I felt like crawling into a shell and staying there forever. But I didn't… and I'm glad I didn't. Because in a few weeks I'd met someone else I liked and, oddly enough, had far more in common with. Sometimes a broken heart is mostly broken pride. But it took a painful experience before I learned this.

"I was about fifteen when I broke up with Bill and for weeks I couldn't eat or sleep. My family pretended not to notice what was wrong with me, but they worried.

"If only a young girl is careful not to let a broken heart make her cynical, she'll gain something valuable every time she loves."

Built in 1912 on the razed site of Nashville's first public school, Hume-Fogg had a reputation, both for its students' athletic prowess and for their scholastic achievements. The school was a looming structure, with an exterior of hard granite reminiscent of the Bastille. According to James C. Armistead, the institution's former coach: "It was a difficult school that took more pride in flunking than passing students."

Fanny studied hard at Hume-Fogg and did well, which naturally pleased her parents – especially the serious-minded Solomon. Her mother, on the other hand, got her greatest joy out of her daughter's artistic achievements, such as her singing, which she continued to practice sans formal training. It wasn't hard to get "that Shore girl" to sing at a school dance or assembly. Indeed, one classmate, Lorraine Regan Thornton would never forget Frances Rose's moving rendition of "Mood Indigo," sung in the school cafeteria during lunchtime, with only a piano accompaniment.

McDowell's Café in Winchester was another spot where Miss Shore could burst into song. She returned to her birthplace every summer to visit relatives and friends for a few weeks. McDowell's was a rural version of Candyland. Kids hung out there on lazy afternoons when they weren't in the mood to go swimming. "It wouldn't take much cajoling to get Dinah to stand up on a table and sing 'Minnie the Moocher,'" said former beau Blevins Rittenberry, a pharmacist in nearby Cowan, Tennessee. "She loved to sing and would do so without any music.

"When she was about fifteen or sixteen, I ran into Dinah on the pier at Daytona Beach, Florida. She was there on vacation with her sister. I coaxed her a little and she got up on the bandstand and started singing for the crowd."

Unlike many Hume-Fogg students who made the mistake of avoiding their teachers, Frances tried to become acquainted with all her instructors: "Some of the cold-seeming teachers were the ones I got to know best. They weren't cold at all. It was just that they had such dignity, such little fortresses of poise! I admired them and wanted to penetrate that reserve. I had to get inside people."

Her favorite school activity was dramatics, a subject taught at Hume-Fogg by Inez Alder, who at one time had had director Delbert Mann (*Marty, Separate Tables*) as a student. For Mrs. Alder, Fanny played leads in such plays as *Outward Bound*, *Little Women* (as "Jo"), and Gilbert and Sullivan's *The Mikado*, a production that revived her vocal ambitions. "She was a splendid actress," recalled the instructor, "very popular with her fellow students, and possessing a quick mind."

Appearing in one of Fanny's shows was Coach Armistead: "They thought it would be fun to have the football coach in the play. I was terrible in the production, but Dinah was great."

The old Orpheum Theater in Nashville, even with oil dripping from its ceiling fan, was a favorite stopping-off point for touring stock companies during the twenties and thirties. A group of actors would present a season of plays on those boards, then, hopefully, move on to greener fields, such as Broadway. Ralph Bellamy spent a season at the Orpheum, as did Shirley Booth.

Fanny Rose and cousin Dodie enjoyed hanging around the theater, watching the professionals at work. Surely the future singing star wished she could take part in those productions. On one occasion, she got the opportunity. The script called for an actor to play the piano, but unfortunately the performer cast in the role didn't know how. Fanny did. Desperate, the show's director drafted her to sit offstage and, on cue, play the desired tune while the actor faked it at a dummy piano. One might say that this was Dinah Shore's debut in the professional theatre.

It was a few days before her high school production of *Little Women* when Frances Rose had what might be considered an *ESP* experience. She was in a class when, unexpectedly, she had a premonition that something was amiss. Leaving her seat, she approached the teacher and said, "I have to go home. There's something terribly wrong with my mother."

"How do you know?" asked the dubious instructor.

"I don't know. I just know that she needs me and that I have to leave."

The teacher asked that Fanny phone home first, just to be sure her imagination wasn't playing games with her. This suggestion was followed and, when the maid answered the phone, the girl was told that her mother had been on her way to play golf when she suffered an attack of indigestion. "I wish you'd come home," pleaded the domestic.

Against her instructor's wishes – she didn't think that an upset stomach was sufficient cause for alarm – Fanny left school. She knew that her mother's ailment was more serious than simple indigestion.

Frances ran all the way home – dreading what she might find when she got there. Pushing open the front door, she ran up the stairs, arriving at her mother's bedside just in time to hold her hand as she died of a heart attack. Handsome and robust Anna Stein Shore was only forty-four years old.

No matter how old a person is when he loses a parent, especially one with whom he'd never had an extremely close relationship, there is always that extra sense of loss beyond the physical: a sentiment which was never spoken, or the feeling of love never expressed. Now, that opportunity had passed forever.

Even though, intellectually, Dinah would come to realize that her mother loved her deeply and had only been harsh so she would develop a sense of self-sufficiency, there were still the vital, if often misconstrued, emotional aspects to deal with: "I never felt that I completely measured up to what Mother was or what she wanted me to be."

"The show must go on," is what they say in the theatre, and fifteen-year-old Frances Rose was not one to break this tradition. Difficult as it might have been, she opened in *Little Women* on schedule, turning in a "fine performance," according to her dramatic coach. Reflected Mrs. Alder: "Watching Fanny out on that stage just after her mother had died was heart-breaking. I was standing in the wings with tears in my eyes."

Alone and with a teenage daughter to raise, Solomon Shore was at a loss. He, of course, loved Frances, but he traveled a lot, supervising his various business interests. What did he know about the emotional needs of this younger generation? Anna had always handled that department – and very well.

He called on Elizabeth, his eldest girl, for assistance. She was now residing in St. Louis with her husband of about one year, Dr. Maurice Seligman, who'd recently completed medical school. For the Seligmans, it had been "love at first sight." They'd met when both were eleven years old.

After discussing the matter, the couple decided they would quit Missouri and move back to Nashville in order to provide a proper home environment for Fanny. It was a major sacrifice, since Maurice had just been given his internship with a chance at a specialty in a major St. Louis hospital; and Bessie was working on her master's degree in child psychology.

This was not the last time the Seligman's would uproot their home in order to look after the younger Miss Shore.

Recalling her sister during this period, Mrs. Seligman told *Redbook* in 1958: "Dinah could never live on her allowance. She drove Daddy wild, charging things. The convertible he gave her for her high school graduation became a family menace. Somebody always had to find it, put in gas and drive it home. She banged a ukulele constantly and left a trail of cast-off clothes all over the house. I suppose you'd have called her a typically vague teenager – only worse, because so many things buzzed around in her head."

The Maurice Seligmans possessed peaceful temperaments, totally contrasting those of the Solomon Shores; hence, Fanny was no longer subjected to the fierce bickering she suffered with her parents: "Like all southern girls, I thought mostly about getting married someday. And I wanted to be married like Bessie and Maurice were," Dinah has said. Her relationship with her brother-in-law was particularly warm and had remained so throughout the years: "I think he understands me better than anyone else. He was patient, always patient, with a crazy mixed-up teenager."

1934 was a memorable year for Nashville. President Franklin D. Roosevelt visited the city, a new million dollar post office was opened, and "Fannye" Rose Shore graduated from Hume-Fogg High School. The school yearbook listed her as a member of the Latin Club, the Dramatic Club, the Music Club, winner of the Girl's Declamatory Contest and, as previously noted, "Best All-Round Girl." The class prophecy predicted she would have a theatrical career and, as her "last will and testament," she left her successors "a lead nickel."

In the fall, Frances enrolled at Nashville's Vanderbilt University, where she majored in Sociology ("That was my people-instinct coming out."), minored in Economics, and became active in just about everything. She was president of her sorority; a member of the Women's Student Government Association board, the Pan Hellenic Council, the Glee Club; and was on the girl's fencing and swimming teams. "I was mighty giddy," she admitted.

"She didn't have a great gift for math," reflected Charles Madison Sarratt, Vanderbilt's Dean of Men and one of Dinah's dearest friends at the college. "Trig was her greatest failing. Her mind was always on other things, and she didn't have the time to stop and think the problems out. Dinah came back to speak at a university assembly during her Chevy years. After she'd finished, I brought out a trig book and started asking questions. She really turned pale."

According to one of her fellow students at Vanderbilt, Miss Shore talked a great deal in class, sometimes distracting the lecturer. One professor even threw a piece of chalk at her. She kept quiet then...briefly.

Her biology instructor was Dr. Claude Chadwick, who remembered that Fanny did above average work in his class: "Plant metabolism, chlorophyll, and photosynthesis were the topics that interested her most." Chadwick was also faculty advisor of the Camera Club, of which Dinah was a member: "Nothing seemed to phase her. At some meetings of the group, she was the only girl present, but that didn't bother her."

Fanny, at first, had fully intended to become a social worker after college – at least until she married and had children – but the lure of a professional singing career was too inviting. Her personal favorites in the music field were Maxine Sullivan, Jimmie Lunceford, and Count Basie.

While she was in her sophomore year, John A. Lewis, her old voice teacher, arranged an audition for her at WSM, a Nashville radio station, whose musical director was Beasley Smith. Years before, Smith also attended Vanderbilt as a pre-med student. Forsaking a life as a doctor, he formed his own orchestra and toured the country from 1923 until 1934, when he retired from the one-night stands and joined the radio station. As a composer, he wrote such tunes as, 'Tennessee Central Number Nine" and "Night Train to Memphis."

The WSM audition was held with Frances unaware that she was being considered for a job. Lewis had thought she might be too nervous to do her best work. As a ruse, he told her she was singing into a dead microphone.

Smith, a shy and gentle man, was impressed with Miss Shore's vocal abilities ("He said I had an unusual style of phrasing. I wasn't sure what he meant by that."). He signed her to appear on a series of fifteen minute shows called "Rhythm and Romance." Her salary was $2.50 per broadcast. Since Father was still paying the bills, it wasn't unusual for the girl to carry her uncashed station checks around with her for weeks.

WSM had several girl singers working for them in the mid-thirties. The station would start them out with only a piano accompaniment, then as their popularity increased, would back them with a small group or orchestra. A few of the shows were even fed into the NBC network.

"Sweet and Hot" was another show Miss Shore did. Airing twice per week, this contrast in musical styles paired the songstress with a gal named Louise Hammett, who sang the "sweet" songs, leaving the "hot" tunes for Dinah.

"She developed her microphone technique at WSM," says Aaron Shelton, one of the station's engineers. "We didn't have electronic modifiers back in those days, so the singers had to know just how close they could stand to the mike for the best pick-up. Dinah became very adept."

Her frequent piano accompanist and good pal at WSM was Owen Bradley: "Dinah gave a dramatic flair to her songs. She always wanted to sing the verse, which I never knew and had to learn. For a guy who thought he was a jazz pianist, that was a bit of a bother."

Both Dinah and Bradley were "spot workers" at the station, meaning that they weren't on staff, but were only utilized as needed. Fortunately, station manager Ollie Riehl had two sisters with whom the singer was close. The girls were always willing to put in a good word for their performing friend. Politicking for an extra show or two per week wasn't beneath Dinah's dignity.

"Dinah was fun to be around and we were always kidding with her," recalled Shelton. "Wednesday nights, after her ten o'clock broadcast, she'd sit in the control room with the crew and listen to 'Lights Out' from the network. That was a big industry hit."

One of the station's commercial arrangements at that time was with Pan American. Every day when the train went through town at around five p.m., WSM would interrupt programming to broadcast the blast of the whistle. And according to Bradley, "Sometimes it would come right in the middle of Dinah's number. She'd be blown right off the air."

"My ambition was to sing in a band," reflected Dinah, "but Daddy made me promise that if I ever got such a job, I wouldn't go on the road with them... He didn't think I was equipped to handle the experiences which might come my way traveling with a band. He thought I was over emotional and therefore vulnerable to designing males; and, looking back, I can see that he knew more about me than I did about myself."

When the opportunity did arise for Fanny to travel one summer with a local dramatic group, Solomon gave his consent only after Bessie agreed to accompany her sister on all out-of-town engagements. (Some time before this, Solomon Shore had forced his daughter to withdraw from the "Miss Centennial Park Pool" beauty contest when he learned that a photo of her clad only in a bathing suit would appear in the newspaper.)

Through her pleasing stylings of popular songs on WSM, Fanny became a local celebrity. She sang at school dances to the music of such visiting orchestra leaders as Kay Kyser, Hal Kemp, and Sammy Kaye, and was even heard on a national broadcast of radio's "Hit Parade" when once it originated from Vanderbilt. Blues numbers being her specialty, her signature tune on "Rhythm and Romance" was a rendition of "Dinah," which she'd pirated from an Ethel Waters record.

Frances, like most people born under the sign of Pisces, was happiest when she was "in love," and there were plenty of romantic opportunities throughout her college career. During the summer before she started at Vanderbilt, she fell hard for a student professor with whom she'd planned to elope to Kentucky. Fortunately, Solomon got wind of her plans, and she promised to wait to have a proper wedding. Once Fanny started school, however, she realized that what she thought was love was merely a "summer flirtation," and promptly ended the relationship.

While in her freshman year, she started going with a sophomore. It was he, in fact, who accompanied her to WSM on the night of her first broadcast. "I was going to sing 'Stars Fell on Alabama,'" she recalled a few years later, "but I didn't get around to learning the words. I had decided to make notes of the lyrics and sing from them, but my date said no, that I wouldn't make a good impression that way. So, for the entire trip to the station he had me repeating the song until I knew it perfectly.

"From then on we were pals. After school we went our separate ways. A few years passed. He joined the Naval Air Corps. One day I received a letter from him, telling me he expected to get a furlough shortly, and would I save a date for him? He wrote that he heard my broadcasts from where he was stationed, so I planned to sing 'Stars Fell on Alabama,' knowing he'd recognize the tune and know it was my way of saying 'yes.'

"Two days before the program went on the air, I received a wire from his mother. He had been killed at Pearl Harbor. And so I didn't sing 'Stars Fell on Alabama.' I never have since."

***

It was the summer between her junior and senior years at Vanderbilt that Fanny, as president of her sorority, journeyed to Vermont to attend a convention. On the way home, she stopped off in New York City to visit a friend and also to see what her prospects were for beginning a professional singing career.

While in Gotham, the aspiring songstress auditioned for and was rejected by both CBS radio and pianist Eddie Duchin's orchestra; met an agent named Lou Mindling, who liked her style and gave her encouragement; and also was helped with some arrangements by a song plugger named Martin "Ticker" Freeman. Though nothing was consummated then, Mr. Freeman would soon become a very important influence in Frances Rose's life.

Somebody suggested to Fanny that she might have better luck finding work if she met the "right people," and the best place to do that was at one of the city's gala cocktail parties, which were attended by many show biz VIP's: "I didn't drink or smoke, but they kept handing me manhattans. I'd set them down here and there. A fellow said, 'You're not drinking.' When he turned his head, I threw the contents of my glass over my shoulder toward a window. It wasn't open. The stuff splashed back, all over my dress. I ran."

Ultimately, Frances auditioned for station music director Jimmy Rich and WNEW. She wrote home to tell her father of the wonderful "break." He was, predictably unimpressed, insisting that she return to Vanderbilt to obtain her degree. "She was in tears when she told me the news," recalled Rich. "But I told her to obey her father – go home, graduate, then come back to New York and see me."

Frances Rose Shore received her Bachelor of Arts degree in 1938 and, although she never went into social work, found her Vanderbilt years most valuable: "College gave me the opportunity to gain poise; it taught me to understand people and to like them; it started friendships that will continue for a long time to come. And it gave me a sense of security I might not have had otherwise."

Her two-month stay in New York had convinced Fanny that she did have a reasonable shot at becoming successful as a singer. After all, with plenty of competition around willing to sing for nothing, why would WNEW have picked her if she didn't have talent? She was determined to try again, but this time something was to be added to her approach.

The song she'd sung at her many auditions the previous year was her old standby, "Dinah." She'd utilized it so much that the station executives at WNEW began referring to her as "that Dinah girl." So, why not take advantage of this? "Dinah Shore" was certainly a charming moniker; was less staid than Frances Rose Shore; and if it aided in her quest for recognition, then that was the important thing.

Hoping to discourage his youngest offspring, Solomon Shore cut off all her charge accounts and her allowance. "Daddy thought what I was trying to do was disgraceful," says Dinah. "To him, only brazen women were in show business."

She was not to be stopped, however. Since grade school her hobby had been photography, and to obtain a stake to sustain herself in New York, she sold her valuable collection of cameras and equipment, as well as several other prized items. Total proceeds: $253.75.

Solomon, who admired singer Gracie Fields and used her as a yardstick to judge all other performers, couldn't understand why his child didn't want to stay in Nashville, marry some nice Jewish boy, and raise a family. Or, at the very least, with her degree in Sociology, get a job doing welfare work.

Yet in his own way, he was a loving father and, reluctantly, he put her on a train for New York. As he kissed her goodbye, he said, "Fanny, there are ten thousand people who can sing well. Are you as good as they?"

With that disturbing question in mind, Dinah Shore went off into the world to seek her fortune.

2.

Radio Days in New York

BACK IN THE THIRTIES AND EARLY FORTIES, WHEN THE BIG BANDS WERE all-powerful, singers out to make names for themselves found that the easiest way to reach their goal was to be hired by one of the more successful instrumental groups. With only a few notable exceptions, nearly every major vocalist to emerge during this period had his or her beginnings with a band.

The life of a band singer was not always an enviable one. Unestablished crooners were often paid less than musicians in the group – primarily because they were in plentiful supply and because there was no union to protect them. Male vocalists, in order to keep their positions secure, would sometimes be forced to do double duty – helping the musicians with their instruments or serving as curator for the music library. As for the girl singers, their additional assignments might be secretarial, or something similar.

There were, of course, problems that applied to both sexes. It was not uncommon, for example, for a songster to be strapped with an arrangement pitched outside his vocal range, having inherited it from an altogether differently toned predecessor. Proper phrasing of a tune's lyrics was another factor often sacrificed in the interest of presenting a more speeded-up tempo, arranged for the dancer, rather than the listener.

Inadequate public address systems, out-of-tune pianos, and overly loud bands were additional curses to the traveling vocalists who, despite the minimum wages they were paid and their miserable life traveling day-in-and-day-out on a crowded, stuffy band bus, were required to look fresh and "pretty as a picture" for each night's performance.

When it came to recording with their particular group, the warblers frequently found themselves handed a new song they'd never seen before and were expected to give it a memorable rendition after only a run-through or two. Few could, and this resulted in many inferior records of tunes that the singers later perfected on the bandstand.

On the plus side, however, the bands gave their singers professional experience. Peggy Lee, a former Benny Goodman chirp, claimed that with the much-heralded group she learned discipline, the value of rehearsal, how to work with musicians and audiences, and ways to deal with band arrangements that didn't quite fit her vocal style.

Frank Sinatra, a Tommy Dorsey graduate, was so impressed with his boss' breath control on the trombone that he began a series of breathing and physical-fitness exercises to improve his own vocal equipment. "The Voice," in fact, considered the time he spent with Dorsey to have been invaluable in developing his professional poise, and recommended that any aspiring singer would do well to begin his career with a large orchestra.

National exposure was a further benefit garnered by big-band vocalists – especially those identified with the more successful groups. The leaders gave their singers a showcase to develop and display their abilities to the paying public, who later made it possible for them to go out on their own.

Band leaders, too, profited when one of their contracted singers began drawing a personal following. Almost always, these performers were on a modest straight salary and received no other financial reward, even when they cut a hit record or lured their own multitude of fans to band engagements. Merv Griffin, for instance, was paid a mere fifty dollars for recording his three-million seller, "I've Got a Lovely Bunch of Coconuts," while leader Freddy Martin got all the royalties.

The Dorseys were quite lucky with their singers. Frank Sinatra crooned "I'll Never Smile Again," "Hear My Song," and "Violetta" for Tommy, while brother Jimmy capitalized on Bob Eberly and Helen O'Connell's "Green Eyes." On the strictly distaff side, Wee Bonnie Baker gave a major boost to Orrin Tucker when she introduced "Oh, Johnny," as did Ella Fitzgerald to Chick Webb with "A-Tisket, A-Tasket." The list of salaried singers who handed their bosses one or more major hits – in some instances making that group's reputation – is virtually endless.

As a vocalist's personal charisma grew to the point where it overshadowed that of the band with which he was affiliated, he understandably tried to break away from the group so he could build his own career and profit fully from his labors. Frequently, such maneuvers were difficult, since the leaders – fearful of losing their major drawing cards – were reticent to release their songsters from long-term, low-paying employment contracts. The bosses argued that these "ingrates" owed them a certain loyalty because they'd been provided the showcase by which the singers had achieved their fame. Conversely, the rebellious vocalists claimed that their talent was being exploited and sometimes misused, yet they were reaping none of the financial benefits.

Leaders attempted to hold their disgruntled singers – with varying degrees of success. Some of the employees worked-out the time; many bought themselves out of their contracts; while others found legal loopholes that allowed their early departure. Legend tells us that one popular crooner got his release after some gangster buddies had a "friendly" chat with his boss and convinced him that enforcing the contract could be dangerous to his health.

When the big bands ultimately declined in popularity, all of the singers were left to their own devices. Some, of course, quickly faded into obscurity, while others like Sinatra, Peggy Lee, Rosemary Clooney, Jo Stafford, and Kay Starr went on to become major recording and nightclub artists in their own right.

For the many vocalists who were not lucky enough to tie-up with a band, getting a decent foothold for a show business career was near impossible. A very few singers – like Kate Smith and Nat "King" Cole – achieved major stardom without such associations, but in most of these instances the artist had "paid their dues" already in other areas of entertainment. Cole, for example, started out as a jazz musician. Miss Smith came from Broadway and vaudeville.

Dinah Shore was another who bypassed the bands. But with Dinah, the maneuver was an involuntary one. Truly, the line of orchestra leaders and talent agents who later admonished themselves for *not* signing this eager young songstress when she auditioned for them back in the late thirties is quite long.

The world was on the threshold of war when the former Frances Rose arrived in New York with her "mammoth" stake of $253.75 (minus train fare), but Neville Chamberlain and his "peace in our time" philosophy and the revolution in Spain were just too far removed for her – or most Americans, for that matter – to be deeply concerned about them now. She had a career to forge.

Variety, in 1938, was talking about Orson Welles' sensational radio broadcast, "The War of the Worlds," which had panicked many listeners into believing that the Earth was being invaded by Martians. Robert Sherwood's moving historical play, *Abe Lincoln in Illinois*, starring Raymond Massey, was being hailed as a modern classic, and the brightest new star on Broadway was a perky young girl from Texas named Mary Martin who stepped out on stage in *Leave It to Me* and stopped the show with her rendition of "My Heart Belongs to Daddy."

Not really knowing the value of a dollar ("There'd always been dollars in my pocket because Daddy put them there.") and having been raised in comfortable surroundings, it was only natural that Dinah would choose to stay at a fairly nice hotel and, for convenience sake, call upon room service frequently. Considering the encouraging reactions she'd received on her previous auditions, it surely wouldn't be very long before she was earning a good salary, so why not live as well as possible?

Things didn't go that smoothly though, as the twenty-one-year-old girl quickly found out. First off, there was the important radio talent agent who agreed to represent her – *only* if she dropped that "corny" name of Dinah. It was just one more ultimatum, like the ones her father had issued the past couple of years to get her to remain in Nashville. She kept her new name.

After that, there were the promised auditions with major bands that never materialized. And those that did – like the ones with Tommy Dorsey and Woody Herman – didn't go very well. "When I first started singing," she recalled, "I tried to be everything but myself. I had my songs over-arranged, and while at the beginning I was never fired, I was just never hired. I was so unsure of myself that sometimes I'd go home from an audition feeling there was nothing left in the world to sing about."

She renewed her acquaintance with handsome Martin "Ticker" Freeman, the song plugger-arranger she'd met in 1937. After he'd accompanied her on the piano for her audition at Leo Feist, the music-publishing firm where he worked, the pair developed a mutual admiration that lasted over two decades. Recalled Freeman: "First time I heard her, I thought she was pretty good for blues and ballads."

Ticker not only helped Dinah come up with better arrangements than she'd been using in her auditions, but also became her personal accompanist, chief adviser, severest critic, and alter ego. "He was the first person in my professional life whom I would let see what mattered to me," Dinah once said. "If I failed an audition – and boy, did I fail them! – I could tell Ticker. I could cry my eyes out. He wouldn't think any less of me. He gave me confidence to go ahead and sing *my* way – be myself. Now I don't know where his style stops and mine begins."

Romance was totally absent from the professional relationship, which was actually more like that of a brother and sister who appreciate each other's faults and virtues. "There was just that one time," according to Freeman, "when we let our hair down a little bit. We'd had a glass of champagne at a studio party and we were driving home. All of a sudden Dinah turned to me and said, 'You know, I'm crazy about you, Ticker.'

"I knew she meant as a pal, of course, and I said, 'I feel the same way about you, Dinah.' Otherwise, we've always skipped the sweet talk."

Aside from joining up with Ticker, the first good break that came Dinah's way was being rehired by Jimmy Rich of station WNEW to sing – again without pay – on various sustaining programs. "Anybody who had any talent interested me," said Rich, "and Dinah had talent. I liked working with young singers, helping them to reach their full potential."

There was another unknown working for no pay on WNEW. He was a young, skinny Italian kid who would very shortly become one of show business' biggest stars. His name was Frank Sinatra.

Dinah had snagged her first commercial program. The sponsor was a New Jersey furniture company that insisted this Hoboken kid share the mike with her. "I didn't see the necessity for Frankie at all," she reflected, "It was *my* show first! And after a few broadcasts, he didn't think I added much to the program – my accent was all wrong, even for South Jersey! We went along like that for a few weeks – and then we got a fan letter...We both jumped on it! And the letter said:

"'I enjoy your program very much, except the love duets. The two kids singing the duets don't seem to like each other.'

"After that, we kinda cooled off.

"I remember Frankie and I were perpetually scared we would lose our jobs and worried that we wouldn't amount to anything," admitted Dinah, who over the years has maintained her friendship with "The Voice." "Frank has fallen lower and risen higher than anybody. His is one of the most unusual talents and most exciting personalities in show business. He's one of a kind, but personally I could never survive in that kind of an atmosphere of constant tension.

"Frank is brilliant. If he were a painter he'd be a great artist, but while he does some of the greatest things in the world, when he explodes he explodes louder than anybody."

Miss Shore was once the cause of a Sinatra burst of anger. So awed was Frank by her ladylike ways, he socked a man for saying a dirty word in her presence.

Were Dinah and Sinatra just good friends, or was there more to their relationship?

According to the late George Jacobs, Sinatra's former valet, in his memoir, *Mr. S: My Life with Frank Sinatra*: "No man has ever slept with so many famous women. Pre-Oscar, the only celebrity I knew to have slept over was Dinah Shore, who was a long-running affair of Sinatra's."

Jacobs did not elaborate.

Dennis Day and Frankie Laine were two other rookie singers who were around during those salad days in New York. One of Dinah's first radio shows, in fact, was with the man who put "Mule Train" and "Moonlight Gambler" on the charts. It was Laine's show, but he was more than happy to turn over his fifth number to the songstress, *if she could cut in.* "When I got to that studio," Dinah remembered, "all those mikes and pointing fingers and clocks and dials and needles made me scared stiff! That's when I used the sweet talk on Frankie, and he was as nice as he could be. He just held my hand the whole time, and when it came time for me to sing, he gave my hand a little squeeze and I clean forgot all those pointing fingers."

Dinah sang for free for almost a year at WNEW, but claims she wouldn't trade the experience for a million dollars. She perfected her use of the microphone and claims "that's worth a mint of money to any singer."

The WNEW job even cost *her* money, since she had to pay $2.50 each for recordings of her programs, so she could sit and listen to them, over and over again, to see how to improve herself: "I found out I was singing too loud. I had to realize that on the radio you should relax and sing popular music softly. The amplifier brings up the volume and the listener gets that soft intimate quality – like somebody was whisperin' a song in his ear."

Spots on WNEW also brought her abilities to the ear of a number of influential people in the music industry. They were impressed with her throaty, dreamy, "fundamentally instinctive" style of singing that she'd ultimately perfected and tagged "noodling" – or "the way Negro mammies in the South sing to their youngsters."

George Simon of *Metronome Magazine* liked her talent and tagged her "the find of the year." Later, the editor of *Down Beat* was also turned-on by what he heard. "I must have had a new style," she told *Saturday Evening Post* in 1959. "I did all my singing in a microphone because I couldn't be heard without one. That in itself was different. The popular women singers of that day, such as Kate Smith, Frances Langford, and Ethel Merman, belted their songs out until they bounced against the walls in the back of a theater. My style of delivery was strictly geared to radio and records."

The Simon review and WNEW producer Vic Knight are credited with getting Dinah an audition, such as it was, with the King of Swing himself, Benny Goodman: "At that point, Benny was doing the Camel Cigarette radio show; he was too busy to listen to me, except during his lunch break, and while I sang for him he had his mouth full of a hot pastrami sandwich. I understand now how frantic things are when you work in radio and TV, but I didn't know then, and seeing his jaws working on a sandwich with my whole future at stake froze my voice in my throat. In fairness to Benny, he may have been thrown by my idea of an attractive costume, for I wore a droopy sweater, a droopier plaid skirt, and scuffed saddle shoes."

By the end of 1938, Dinah had had plenty of exposure via WNEW, plus some brief club engagements with the likes of bandleaders Mitch Ayres, Johnny Gart, and Peter Dean. The Dean gig had come about through the influence of George Simon, who'd been introducing her to various music people around town. Dean and his fifteen-piece group were then being heard live from Nick's in Greenwich Village every week over NBC.

Peter Dean: "Dinah came in and auditioned with 'How Come You Do Me Like You Do, Do, Do.' She was great and I hired her." Her salary was seventy-five dollars per week, but the engagement was a temporary one, lasting only two weeks.

With only sporadic paying jobs, Dinah's financial situation was bleak. She had moved several times into progressively cheaper living quarters until she was sharing a thirteen dollar per week one-room apartment with four other girls: "The other girls lived much better than I did because they always seemed to have lots of dinner dates. I don't know what was the matter with me, but no one ever bought me an English muffin." Her food budget was thirty-five cents per day, which meant she survived on drugstore sandwiches.

New Year's Eve – 1938: Dinah was dead-broke. She was singing at WNEW – still for free – when the staff organist received a call. A girl singer was needed for an orchestra that was playing at an all-night party. Being a good pal, the musician turned the information over to Dinah who, when she learned they were paying twenty-five dollars, jumped at the opportunity and rushed home to get ready.

She was ecstatic as she prepared that afternoon for the engagement. The job seemed heaven-sent, and who could tell? Possibly there'd be an important Broadway producer in the crowd who'd sign her for his next big musical show. She borrowed a pretty cocktail dress from one of her roommates, ironed it, and just about the time she'd slipped it on, there was a phone call for her. It was her organist friend. The party had been cancelled and the people apologized if she'd been put to any special trouble.

Dinah was devastated. She was alone – without money or prospects – in the impersonal city of New York on December 31st. What could be more depressing than watching happy couples rushing to gay restaurants and parties on that night of merriment? According to *Time* (10/19/42), she briefly considered ending it all. But she took hold of herself. Though she'd failed there were still other things in life besides singing.

In tears, Dinah borrowed a nickel from the elevator operator of her apartment building and made a call to Nashville – collect. "Daddy," she said, "I haven't any money to buy food. Please wire me money so I can eat – and come home."

Bessie and Maurice Seligman were visiting Solomon that New Year's Eve, and Dinah could hear her sister in the background saying something to their father. A few moments later, Solomon surprised the sobbing girl with his reply: "Singing's the thing you like best, honey, and the thing you want to do. I'll wire you money, but don't let those Yankees say a Nashville girl ever quit. You stay there and fight it out. Next year's bound to be better."

Sister had come through for Dinah again. She'd used her psychology training to persuade Solomon that the worst thing he could do would be to force Dinah to come home before she'd proved herself.

***

Things changed for the better after the first of the year. Early in January, Dinah was signed to sing with orchestra leader Leo Reisman for a two-week engagement at the Strand Theater. The show played on the same bill with a John Garfield movie, *They Made Me a Criminal*. Known for his melodic, society-styled dance music, Reisman had gained his reputation in the twenties through a series of radio broadcasts from the Central Park Casino. He gave starts to Ned Brandwynne and Eddie Duchin, and on some of his recordings he featured vocalists like Harold Arlen, Lee Wiley, and Fred Astaire.

During her brief appearance with the leader, Dinah was called upon to sing one number for each show. Halfway through the performance, she'd warble a quick chorus of "Won't You Hurry Home," and for this she received the sum of seventy-five dollars per week. She got an advance on her first week's salary and spent it on a huge meal of fried chicken, candied yams and mince pie. Unfortunately, the rest of that week's pay was stolen from her dressing room.

Dinah received quite a surprise when she walked out on to the Strand stage for one of her performances. Sitting in the front row was her father. Solomon had flown up from Nashville to see his daughter, and he beamed his approval.

Said *Variety* of her appearance: "…the gal vocalist is on for a single song. Nicely gowned, she sells a song passably and has an unaffected ease of manner, but doesn't pile up much of a wallop for the windup."

She signed a contract to go on the road with Reisman to Texas, and then announced the fact to her mentor, Jimmy Rich. "Dinah had a mania for signing these contracts without seeking advice first," reflected Rich. "I told her to get out of the Reisman contract, and she did. If she'd gone to Texas, that would have been the last anybody would have heard of her.

"Another thing she used to do was go out and have publicity pictures taken. They were always unusable. I was constantly bawling her out for doing it."

There were other well paying jobs on the horizon. Xavier Cugat, the colorful former violinist with Phil Harris' band who later formed his own popular Latin-American group, had caught her act at the Strand and hired her to cut an album with his Waldorf-Astoria orchestra for RCA Victor. "Dinah was strictly an American singer and I was Latin," recalled Cugat, "which was the whole idea of the album. We wanted to combine a Latin sound with English lyrics."

Some of the tunes Dinah sang with "Cugie" on their project were "Whatever Happened to You," "Jungle Drums," "La Cumparsita," "Quiereme Mucho," and the best-known of the efforts, "The Thrill of a New Romance." Her pay was approximately twenty-five dollars per number.

She was a bundle of nerves during that recording session, and when the sound engineer spoke to her she wasn't really listening. "Is your name 'Dinah Shaw?'" he asked. Dinah nodded, unaware of his error.

To record collectors, that initial pressing of "Romance" with Dinah's misspelled credit is now a prized item and said to be worth a "small fortune."

Sometime after the Cugat records started to appear, Dinah got a recording deal of her own – with Bluebird – and did several discs, accompanied by artists like Leonard Joy, Paul Weston (in one of his first recording sessions), and Dick Todd. Among the songs she recorded: "Careless," "Darn that Dream," "I've Got My Eyes on You," "Imagination," "Smoke Gets in Your Eyes," and "The Nearness of You." ("Daddy bought 'em. For a long time I don't think anybody else did.")

In *Metronome*, George Simon was heaping praise on Miss Shore's discs. "A really mellow mood, as created by the year's best new voice" was his comment on "I Thought About You." And of "Smoke Gets in Your Eyes," he said: "The most relaxed side by this wondrous lass who doesn't strain on a difficult tune the way so many other singers do."

Near the end of 1939, Dinah got her first important club date. She appeared with Paul Whiteman and his orchestra in the Terrace Room of the Hotel New Yorker.

Radio work began to be a paying proposition for the Tennessee lass. Hearing that "the Ol'Maestro," Ben "Yow-sah" Bernie, was seeking a new songstress for his American Tobacco Company program on CBS, she decided to audition. But upon arriving at the production office, she found it crowded with several other aspiring singers. Dinah had been to these "cattle calls" before, so she sat down and, to pass the time, began to read a book on semantics she'd just checked out of the library. Sitting next to her was a gentleman who seemed to take an interest in the volume, and the two struck up a conversation. As it turned out, the man had a lunch date with the executive in charge of auditioning singers. He asked Dinah to join them, which she did. Afterwards she was given a preferential audition, and was hired.

The position paid seventy-five dollars per week, and she sang one song per show. Regrettably, it didn't last beyond the first couple of broadcasts: "We got our paychecks from a fabulous 'off-with-her-head' character named George Washington Hill. He was president of the American Tobacco Company and he sat home with Mrs. Hill and tuned in on us and made violent and copious notes of what was wrong with everybody who worked for him. According to him, I didn't sing loud enough or fast enough, so when he commanded, 'Get her off of there!' people fell over themselves firing me."

Mr. Hill got his comeuppance, however. A year later, Dinah was sought out by the American Tobacco Company to make a single appearance on one of their shows. She agreed, but not before they paid her a staggering fee of twenty-five hundred dollars.

Following her quick departure from CBS, she was hired – for money – by NBC as a "sustaining" singer on that network's various variety shows. She could thank Peter Dean for getting her that spot. So impressed was the band leader with the job she did for him at Nick's, he persuaded his friend Ginger Johnson of NBC to come down to the Village and hear her. Johnson liked her style. A few months later, he signed her.

Jimmy Rich: "Dinah was so excited when she told me she'd signed with the network. I asked her how the contract was. She said she hadn't read it. It was too thick. Luckily, everything turned out okay on that deal."

Eventually, Dinah was given her own half-hour program on Sunday nights – opposite the ever-popular Jack Benny show. ("I might as well have been singing into a dead mike.") And yet, listener polls and fan letters indicated that Dinah did have a steady – if small – audience that preferred her show over the comedian's.

Tommy Dorsey had been one of Dinah's listeners and wired her from the Midwest, suggesting that she bolt her NBC deal and come join his band. Her friends – including George Simon, who felt the network staff musicians and arrangers were giving her terrible backings – urged her to accept. Perhaps she was following the advice of Jimmy Rich when she replied, "Nothing doing. I'm on radio now. There's a much better future for me here on my own. If I don't make good with Tommy, there's no telling where I'll wind up."

To pick up extra money, she put in some time at the RCA Exhibit Building at the New York World's Fair, demonstrating the "miracle of the future" – television. At a later Fair engagement, Dinah had the opportunity to meet her "favorite musician," Ferde Grofe ("Grand Canyon Suite") who was conducting the New World Ensemble in daily concerts at the Ford Motor Pavilion.

***

"The Chamber Music Society of Lower Basin Street" was a radio show that featured swing music with a tongue-in-cheek commentary by Gene Hamilton in an antiquated style, and was dedicated to "the three B's: boogie-woogie, barrelhouse, and blues." Debuting over the NBC Blue network in February 1940, the program would feature the orchestras of Paul La Valle (one of the show's creators) and Henry Levine, with the vocal talents of Lena Horne, Diane Courtney, Jane Pickens and Dinah Shore.

Dinah was one of the first ladies to appear as a regular on this memorable series. She was billed as "Mlle. Dinah Diva Shore, who starts fires by rubbing two notes together."

"Dinah was very popular around the network," reflected LaValle. "She was enthusiastic and untiring about everything. We had a swing woodwind group on the show – 'the Woodwindy Ten' – that was great accompaniment for her."

The songstress became the darling of *le jazz hot*; recorded a six-sided RCA album with the show's musicians ("Mood Indigo," "Muskrat Ramble," "Runnin' Wild," "Dinah's Blues," "Shoemaker's Holiday," and "Basin Street Blues" were the numbers); and started garnering critical comments: "The Metropolitan would call her 'vibrato'; Tin Pan Alley would call her 'schmaltzy.'"

Yet, what won her the Radio Editors Award as "The Outstanding New Star of the Year," was most likely the fact that listeners found refreshing her simple, direct and sincere style that was not hampered by the gimmicks many of her contemporaries were employing.

Guest of honor on one of the early "Lower Basin Street" shows was composer William C. Handy, and after hearing the singer's rendition of his "Memphis Blues," he commented, "Miss Shore, that song was never really sung before."

Among others who did the show were Louis Armstrong, Duke Ellington, Jose Iturbi (playing Boogie), and opera star Lauritz Melchior, singing "In the Blue of the Night." According to LaValle, Zero Mostel made his radio debut on the program, doing a comedy bit. "The concept was a spoof, but the music we played was on the level. It was the number-one musical show for a long time, but because of some of the advent-garde jazz we presented was too far out, we were on the air three years before we got a sponsor."

Dinah no longer shared a room with four other girls. Instead, she was living in a large Forest Hills apartment with the blissful Seligmans and their two children – Linda Ann, age five, and John, fourteen months. Bessie and Maurice had recently moved to New York to be close to Dinah, and they were providing her with the kind of stable home atmosphere she relished. ("First, Bessie and Maurice have got a sense of values, and second, they've got unselfishness. He likes symphony music, so sister *learns* to like it.")

She took up photography again and, when she wasn't working, would stalk her little nephew and niece with her Kodak.

Dinah was dating regularly, and most of the guys she saw were either musicians or servicemen. Almost daily, this eternal romantic would announce – usually to Ticker – that she was "in love." The accompanist tired of her constant infatuations and, on one occasion, informed the lady that he thought her beau was a phony. Irked at the remark, she stormed out of the studio and didn't talk to Freeman for over a month. When she learned that the soldier in question had married somebody else, Dinah apologized to her dear friend and the matter was forgotten.

There's an unsavory element found in all aspects of show business that preys on talented – and not so talented – newcomers who have not yet learned the ropes. Willing to give all to anyone they think can help them achieve their dreams of stardom, these novices will often enroll in phony dramatic schools or sign away large percentages of future income to shady agents and personal managers. Such was the case with Dinah.

Virtually everyone she was dealing with – including her hairdresser and the radio network – had claim to a percentage of the naïve singer's earnings when Dr. Seligman called Henry Jaffe, who was then an attorney for the American Federation of Radio Artists, and asked him for his help. "Dinah wanted to please everyone," recalled Jaffe. "When I met her, she had at least four managers, because she couldn't say no. She had herself carved up in so many pieces that she owned about ten percent of herself. I had to call the managers all in and have a little talk."

Jaffe rescued her from the complex legal tangle and, as a result, became her lawyer. He was influential in directing her career ever since.

1940 was an even busier year than the previous one for Dinah. She signed to make guest appearances on radio shows like "The Schaefer Review" and "Raymond Paige's Musical Americana," then played a date at New York's Paramount Theater. ("I saw my name up in lights – on Broadway, mind you!") Though she was now being heard several times weekly on radio, on records, and in occasional public appearances, Miss Shore had not yet broken through as a performer of major stature. But, that transition, which would involve Dinah in radio's Golden Age of Comedy, was about to be made.

3.

Eddie Cantor

IF ONE GENRE OF RADIO PROGRAM FLOURISHED ABOVE ALL THE REST DURING the wireless' Golden Age (the Great Depression through World War II), it was the comedy show. Relying totally on witty words – and mental pictures conjured by the listeners' imaginations – the nation's cleverest funnymen created a unique form of audio humor, which disappeared with the advent of television. Dinah Shore was fortunate to have been a small part of that wonderful era.

The man most responsible for elevating Dinah to major stardom was a performer who did well in both the audio and video mediums. He was slight-of-build, banjo-eyed Eddie Cantor, rated by most entertainment historians as a show business immortal – one of the greatest, most generous entertainers of his day.

Born Israel Iskowitz in 1893 on New York's lower East Side, Cantor was orphaned at the age of two. He grew up under the care of his maternal grandmother, Esther, who managed a haphazard domestic employment agency.

While many of his friends in this poor neighborhood spent their time picking pockets, Eddie sought and found the comic, singing and clowning on street corners for pennies. At fourteen, he met the girl who was to become his inspiration, Ida Tobias. With her encouragement, he braved singing on amateur night at Miner's Bowery Theater, where he won five dollars and began his career as Edward Cantor, singer and impersonator.

Later, on Coney Island, he made a living as a singing waiter, eventually joining Jimmy Durante as a blackface in vaudeville. In 1912, Cantor's rousing rendition of Irving Berlin's "Rag Time Violin" prompted Gus Edwards to give him a major part in the stage show *Kid Kabaret*. Two years later, he was in London in Charlot's *Not Likely*. Honeymooning with Ida during this engagement, Eddie returned home when the United States entered into the World War I and did his part by helping to sell Liberty Bonds and by entertaining the American Expeditionary Forces.

Skipping around the stage and singing with palms outstretched, he captivated Ziegfeld audiences in the *Follies* of 1917, 1918, and 1919. Then, after a quarrel with Ziegfeld, he worked for other producers in such shows as *The Midnight Rounders* and *Make It Snappy*. By 1923, he'd patched up his differences with the great showman, and the pair had major hits with *Kid Boots* and later, *Whoopee* (1928).

Movies beckoned to Cantor. Following starring parts in a couple of silent efforts, *Kid Boots* (1926) and *Special Delivery* (1927), as well as a role in *Glorifying the American Girl* 1929), an early film musical to which Ziegfeld lent his name for promotional purposes, the comedian went under contract to Samuel Goldwyn. For that producer, he starred in several musical-comedy pictures – *Palmy Days* (1931), *The Kid From Spain* (1932), *Roman Scandals* (1933), and *Kid Millions* (1934) – most of which did quite well at the box office. Two subsequent films – for 20th Century-Fox and Metro-Goldwyn-Mayer – bombed, prompting Eddie to quit Hollywood for a while and return to New York – and to radio.

In 1931, he had made his radio debut on Rudy Vallee's program, subsequently starring in his own show a few months later. Then in 1940,

Young and Rubican, the advertising agency handling the Bristol Meyers Company (Ipana, Sal Hepatica), decided to sponsor a second program in addition to their successful Fred Allen show. This move brought Eddie back into radio broadcasting, after being sidelined by the demands of his motion picture activity. (Actually, a year earlier, Cantor had been doing a show for Camels, but after he made a controversial political speech in which he blasted a couple of Nazi sympathizers, his program was cancelled.)

According to Harry von Zell, who wound-up as Cantor's announcer-straight man: "The advertising agency executive who handled Ipana didn't really care for Fred Allen's show, and urged his organization to sponsor the show with Eddie. Being under contract to the agency, I was assigned to work on this new program." (Later, Cantor would be sponsored by Pabst Blue Ribbon Beer.)

In putting together his new entry, which would debut October 2, 1940 over NBC's Red Network, Cantor engaged Cookie Fairchild's orchestra; his old stooge, Bert "The Mad Russian" Gordon; then began seeking a new female vocalist – hopefully one whom he could groom to stardom, as he'd done with Deanna Durbin and Bobby Breen.

Marjorie Cantor, who worked with her father on many of his entertainment endeavors, had heard the Xavier Cugat-Dinah Shore recording of "The Thrill of a New Romance." She suggested that the comic audition this refreshing new singer for the position. "Daddy, this is the girl!" announced a very excited Marjorie halfway through Dinah's first audition number. But, Eddie didn't need to be told. He'd been around a long time and had a keen eye for fine talent. "The minute she opened her pan," he recalled, "I knew. . . I just kept her singing."

"Dinah got nervous when Dad made her do more than a couple of songs," said Marilyn Cantor Baker, another of the comedian's daughters. "She thought she'd flunked the audition. Dad had to assure her that he liked what he heard."

As far as Cantor was concerned, Dinah possessed the most natural singing voice he'd heard since Nora Bayes: she breathed properly; knew proper phrasing; and, unlike many of her contemporaries, understood the meaning of the lyrics. Yet, the most important thing to Cantor was that she was singing not because she was being paid, but because she loved doing it.

Cantor signed her, then proceeded to develop his newest discovery into a major star. His first step was to "glamorize" the still-naïve Tennessee girl. Dinah had a gap in her front teeth filled, at his suggestion. She had already visited a plastic surgeon to have her nose made "more attractive." Additionally, Cantor insisted that the singer have a new wardrobe, one better suited to the more stylish image he wanted her to present to the world.

"Yes, My Darling Daughter" was a sharp new song earmarked for Judy Garland, but Eddie bought the piece for Dinah and had her introduce it on his opening show. Recalled Harry von Zell: "On that program, the audience made her do three encores, which was unusual, considering radio's time factor."

Dinah later recorded the tune for Bluebird and it became her first major hit, selling over a half million discs. ("Its success made me relax a little. Not inside, but outside I stopped trying to be so frantic in front. I found out it was more important to sing to a lot of people and make them feel good than to get the same feeling myself.")

"I never knew anybody who worked so hard," said Eddie to interviewers. "Every week she shows up with twenty new songs. She's rehearsed 'em and she's learned 'em, and she wants to sing all twenty of 'em so I can pick out *one* for the show. She might as well be my sixth daughter – that's how strongly I feel about Dinah."

Cantor was an astute showman, and he was aware that Dinah was a major asset to his program, which unfortunately aired on Wednesday nights opposite Fred Allen's highly-rated entry. "Banjo-eyes" was running second in the competition until he came up with the idea of learning the exact timing of Allen's program. After that, whenever Allen broke for a commercial, Eddie would stick Dinah in front of the mike. People spinning their dials to avoid the commercials would hear her and stay with NBC for the rest of the half-hour. Eventually, Allen insisted that CBS switch him to another night.

Harry von Zell: "The Cantor show was a pleasant, easy show to do. We'd rehearse the script mid-morning on the day we did the program, then Dinah, Eddie, and any singing guests would go over their numbers with the orchestra. Occasionally, Eddie would call a special rehearsal to help the movie-star guests with the sketches, but it was a pretty relaxed atmosphere. We would actually do two broadcasts – one for the East Coast and a later one for the West.

"Dinah came off very well on the program and quickly became adept at responding to the generous ad-libbing that was always going on. She also learned that she had to dress very carefully on this show, since, without warning, Eddie would occasionally pick her up and whirl her around over his shoulders as if she were an adagio dancer.

"He was a bundle of energy and, as a surprise, would – while we were on the air – just jump into my arms. He tried that once with guest Errol Flynn when we were doing a show from Boston. Errol was caught completely off guard and the two of them fell into the audience."

It was while she was with Cantor that Dinah had one of her few brief bouts with illness. Just prior to airtime, she informed her boss that she had laryngitis, to which Eddie replied that he would seek a replacement for her that night. "Never in medical science," remembered the comedian in 1954, "has there been such a fast recovery. She got well so fast and sang so good that she never had laryngitis again."

Marilyn Cantor Baker: "One piece of advice Dad gave Dinah was to *never* run in a full gown. It wasn't dignified. She should pick up her skirt and walk off stage like a lady.

"She was appearing for a week at the Paramount Theater, and Dad took me to see the show. We were sitting in the mezzanine. At the end of her act, Dinah started to run off stage. 'Don't run, Dinah!' Dad said under his breath. It was like she'd heard him. She stopped, and then *walked* off. Later, when we saw her in her dressing room, she explained, 'I suddenly felt I was doing the wrong thing'."

With Eddie behind her, Dinah was rapidly moving up the ladder: the funnyman had acquired movie rights to Al Jolson's Broadway show *Hold on to Your Hats* and was planning to film it with her as the star; there were more records hits: "I Hear a Rhapsody," "Jim," but "Blues in the Night" solidified Dinah's position in the record business. Ticker Freeman had been against her recording that song; he didn't think it could become a hit. But Dinah secretly recorded it, and later, whenever Ticker questioned a tune she liked, she would begin humming, "My Mama done tol' me..."

Columnists began tagging Dinah the "Tennessee Thrush" or the "Southern Songbird"; magazines and various clubs and societies labeled her everything from the "Best Female Vocalist" to "The Girl with the Brightest Smile"; and the offers, including one to join Edgar Bergen's radio show, continued to pour in. By late 1941, NBC had given her her own fifteen-minute radio show. She also remained a regular with Cantor.

The songstress began headlining her in-person engagements at New York area movie houses. She even accepted an offer of one thousand dollars per week to appear at the prestigious Wedgewood Room of the Waldorf-Astoria Hotel.

Then it happened.

Just when Dinah was beginning to truly enjoy her new success, an ugly and completely unfounded rumor began to circulate. Where and how it started, nobody really knew *then*, but considering the racist mentality that prevailed through much of the country during the early forties, the story could have destroyed her career.

Essentially, the lie proposed that Dinah Shore was a black girl *passing* as white. As "evidence," it pointed to her dark hair, southern accent, and that "Dinah" was an unusual name for a Caucasian. Outside of photographs, only a small segment of her public had ever seen her – another factor that added fuel to the rumors.

The American people are not stupid and they, therefore, did not buy this ridiculous falsehood, the memory of which has, strangely, persisted throughout the years. Certainly her fan-following was not significantly affected, because – even if a few of her devotees did choose to listen to the yarn – they either dismissed it as total hogwash, or decided it didn't make any difference, one way or another.

Where did the untruth begin? According to close friends of Miss Shore, she later learned one of her rivals; a vindictive woman singer of that time who Dinah had surpassed in popularity started it. Jealous of the younger songstress, the performer, who was, apparently, thoroughly disliked by her business associates, manufactured the lie in a vain attempt to get rid of her competition. Seemingly, the plan backfired, for today one seldom hears of this once quite popular vocalist...whose name was Kate Smith.

4.

Love and the Movies

NINETEEN FORTY-ONE WAS THE YEAR THAT CUPID MADE HIS SERIOUS entry into Dinah's life – shooting the lady with his arrow while she played an engagement with Milton Berle in an Atlantic City movie theater. Between performances, she caught the film – a forgettable little effort entitled *The Cowboy and the Blonde,* starring George Montgomery. Unimpressed with the picture, but intrigued by its tall, handsome leading man, Dinah sat through the entertainment several times: "I never got so tired of watching any one thing in my life as I did that film." But she confessed to a girl friend who accompanied her on one of the viewings, "That guy is for me."

A few days later Dinah, who'd talked the theater manager into giving her a poster from the film, read in a Hollywood gossip column that Montgomery was engaged to an ultra-glamorous movie star. "What a pity," was her reaction. "I wonder how he's going to get out of this. But he will."

"Go ahead and dream," chuckled her friend.

"This is no dream," she replied prophetically.

***

In the last half of 1942, Dinah was in Hollywood working on her first motion picture, *Thank Your Lucky Stars,* an entertaining all-star revue from Warner Brothers that featured most of the studio's current crop of contract players including, among others, Humphrey Bogart, Bette Davis, Errol Flynn, Olivia de Havilland, Ida Lupino, Dennis Morgan, John Garfield, Ann Sheridan, and Jack Carson, performing a variety of songs and sketches. Eddie Cantor was also in the cast, playing a dual role – himself and a look-alike tour bus driver.

The Mark Hellinger production had been designed with both Cantor and Dinah in mind and, for the six weeks it was filming, the New Yorkers broadcast their individual radio shows from the West Coast.

David Butler, the picture's director, recalled, "The major problem with this movie was scheduling. All the stars were working on other projects and we had to adjust the filming of their brief musical scenes to a time when they might be free. Cantor always felt the script, which revolved around a show-business benefit, needed attention, and regularly called morning conferences with the writers to work on it. He was a lovable, but fussy guy.

"Dinah also portrayed herself. She immediately grasped everything anybody told her. She was excellent at lip-syncing her pre-recorded songs, and usually did them with a minimum of takes."

Although they'd wanted to capitalize on her tremendous popularity as a recording artist, the brothers Warner had, initially, been hesitant about utilizing Miss Shore in the film – mainly because they had doubts that she would photograph well. Thus, upon her arrival at the studio, Dinah, who'd always been insecure about her looks, was turned over to a crew of makeup experts. They proceeded to reshape her nose, mouth, and eyebrows; then they lightened her hair and tried seventeen different styles on it. Frustrated at being treated like a piece of clay, she viewed the artists' finished masterpiece, then went to the sink and washed everything off. The experts were horrified. When she returned to the makeup chair, she said, "There's my mouth. Those are my eyes. That's my nose. Let's go along with *them*, okay?"

"It was a great lesson to me," she reflected years later, "but one I had to teach myself. Standing out there in front of those cameras I kept repeating, 'if they like me this time it's because they like *me* – what they see *and* what they hear – not something I'm pretending to be. And they did like me.

"Then the most amazing thing happened. All of a sudden I had enough confidence in my appearance to stop thinking about it."

One idea the make-up people devised for Dinah, and which she adopted, was the changing of her hair: "I had no talent for doing my hair. It was straight as a poker and my permanents were always too curly, so I used to part it in the middle and bring it straight back. The studio taught me how to bleach it and wear it a different way, and I think this change has been most helpful."

Singing the title tune and numbers called "The Dreamer" and "How Sweet You Are," Dinah came off quite well in *Thank Your Lucky Stars*, yet it was Bette Davis, warbling the now classic "They're Either Too Young or Too Old," and Errol Flynn, with his novelty song, "That's What You Jolly Well Get," who stopped the show. Though not too impressed with the movie, the *New York Times* called it: "…a conventional all-star show which has the suspicious flavor of an 'amateur night' at the studio. But at least it's lively and genial."

Dinah was too timid to attend the sneak preview of *Stars*. Instead, she drove her car to a parking lot near the theater and sat it out. After receiving positive reports from friends, she caught the movie at a studio screening.

Warners announced they were putting Dinah under contract and that two starring vehicles were being readied for her. The first was *Shine On Harvest Moon*, in which she would portray Nora Bayes, to be followed by *Mississippi Belle*, a *Show Boat*-like musical with a Cole Porter score. That was the last anybody ever said about the contract. It was never signed. Ann Sheridan played Nora Bayes. The Porter project was shelved. Dinah Shore never made another movie at Warner Brothers.

The reason the deal fell through was never really made clear, although one rumor claimed that studio brass were disappointed with the way Dinah photographed in a color test for *Shine On Harvest Moon*, and decided to pass on utilizing her services further.

With other movie offers on the horizon and Cantor deciding that he preferred living in the Los Angeles area, Miss Shore also decided to abandon New York, and rented a large comfortable house, which she shared with three other girls – radio actress Shirley Mitchell; her secretary, "Rufus" Crane; and singer Kitty Callan. It was a home constantly filled with visitors – mostly from the radio world – who would come by for dinner or just drop over to enjoy pleasant company.

Next-door neighbor Orson Welles wandered into the place one day around Christmas and was rather amused at the flurry of activity. Dinah was baking cookies, Shirley was wrapping presents, and the other girls were trimming the tree. Finally, the boy genius of Hollywood paused, hands behind his back, and in those deep dramatic tones exclaimed, "Oh, to be young again!"

From that moment, Orson's words became the "lament" of the household. The girls moaned it every morning when the alarm went off.

Dinah and Eddie did their respective shows from the NBC studios, which were then located in Hollywood at the intersection of Sunset and Vine. Bert Gordon had made the trek west with them (and even did a gag appearance in *Thank Your Lucky Stars*), as had Harry von Zell, who remembered: "I became the announcer for Dinah's Sunday night show, as well as continuing with Eddie on Wednesday. She had no trouble getting guests. In fact, Dinah was so well-liked that many major stars, who refused to do other radio programs, would appear with her.

"I would sometimes drive her to the Sunday night show and, during the break between doing the East and West Coast performances, we'd grab something to eat at a nearby hamburger joint. I always had onions on my patty. Dinah didn't, at first, then later, in self-defense, she ordered onions too.

"Although she took her work seriously, she was always warm and friendly to the people she dealt with. She was never cold or aloof, or even reflected a bad state of mind."

Concurrent with the October 1943 release of *Thank Your Lucky Stars*, Dinah found herself doing a new half-hour show on NBC, sponsored by General Foods. Said *Variety* of the debut: "Miss Shore, already recognized as a torcher, proves she has become one of the top emotional-ballad singers. Moreover, in this new series of her own, she is a suave, assured and warmly ingratiating M.C. She has, beyond a doubt, arrived."

Glenhall Taylor, who directed the radio program, found that his star had one fault – a holdover from her high school days: "She was almost always late for rehearsal. She'd come in with a batch of home-made cookies for the crew and explain that she'd just taken them out of the oven. That was her excuse for the delay."

Taylor still shuddered when he recalled the night that Dinah got ill during a broadcast and had to leave the stage in the middle of a number: "Harry von Zell ran up to the mike and sang the last few bars."

Dinah dated a number of men during those early days in Hollywood, including Jimmy Stewart and director Mervyn LeRoy. Nevertheless, there was always the memory of that good-looking piece of beefcake whom she'd viewed a year or so before in *The Cowboy and the Blonde*.

The first time she actually saw the suave, attractive George Montgomery in the flesh was at the Los Angeles Shrine Auditorium, where she was doing a Gershwin concert with Bing Crosby. Peeking through a hole in the curtain, she spotted the star coming down the aisle with Kay Williams, his current girlfriend, and commented to Bing, "That's the man I'm going to marry. Gosh, he knows a lot of beautiful women."

The songstress finally met George on an evening when she was singing for servicemen at the Hollywood Canteen. After finishing her number on the bandstand, she asked the bandleader what other stars were working that night. "Well, let's see," pondered the musician, "George Montgomery's a busboy. Know him?"

He was across the room, his six-foot frame leaning against the kitchen door as he devoured a ham sandwich. The accommodating bandleader made the proper introductions and the chemistry between the couple was immediately apparent to them. They left the Canteen together that evening, had dinner at The Players restaurant, then danced to the music of Emil Coleman at the Mocambo. Dinah got home at five the next morning. From that moment, she knew that it was only a matter of time before she would become Mrs. George Montgomery. Her attraction to him was understandable, for George Montgomery wasn't the kind of man one expects to find in the movie capital.

His real name was George Montgomery Letz, and he was born on August 29, 1916 in rural Montana. The son of Russian immigrants, George was the youngest of fourteen children. "Where I lived," he remembered, "you could hear a horse a quarter of a mile off."

By the time George was ready to begin high school, the family had settled on a ranch near Great Falls. He participated in both football and baseball in school, then, following graduation, studied interior decorating at the University of Montana, where he became a collegiate heavyweight boxing champion for the areas of Montana, Idaho, Washington, and Oregon.

Montgomery could very well have become a professional fighter had he not visited his brother Mike in Hollywood during the summer following his sophomore year. Recognizing that his younger sibling's extreme good looks might win him a career in the movies, the elder Letz introduced George to a man he knew at Metro-Goldwyn-Mayer, who got him a job as a double, riding a horse down a cliff and earning $16.50 for the day.

That was Montgomery's only show-biz job for six months. He earned his livelihood while waiting for studio jobs by working as a carpenter in the construction of a Russian nightclub. Finally, Mike got him in at Republic Pictures, and George began doubling for The Lone Ranger in a 1938 serial of the same name. The director even gave him a line to say – "Here come the rustlers!" – after which he was killed-off in the fifth chapter.

Curiously, Republic received considerable fan mail on this bit player, prompting them to take a closer look at him. The puzzle was quickly explained when they discovered that all the letters were postmarked from either Los Angeles or Great Falls, Montana – George's home town. It seems that friends and relatives had taken pencil in hand, and…

Late in 1939, Twentieth Century-Fox signed the actor with the idea of using him in a series of program westerns. Once they'd convinced him to change his name to, simply, George Montgomery, he was cast in such efforts as *Cisco Kid and the Lady*, with Cesar Romero; *Star Dust*, starring Linda Darnell; and a Shirley Temple vehicle, *Young People*. His first leading role, however, was opposite Carole Landis in *Cadet Girl* (1941), a pre-World War II propaganda movie. The studio publicity department trumpeted the fact that two teenage girls from Los Angeles – unrelated to the performer – had left the theater after viewing *Cadet Girl* and had kissed Montgomery's picture on the lobby card.

This incident made the studio realize George's potential and, once he'd completed previously-assigned roles in *Riders of the Purple Sage,* and Dinah's "favorite," *The Cowboy and the Blonde*, they immediately cast him as Ginger Rogers' love interest in *Roxie Hart* (1942), following it with pivotal parts in *Orchestra Wives*, a Glenn Miller vehicle; *Ten Gentlemen from West Point*, starring Maureen O'Hara; *Coney Island*, with Betty Grable; and *China Girl*, which for many years he considered his favorite film.

"When I was given the part in *China Girl*," Montgomery said, "I was puzzled as I was pleased. Frankly, I thought the role was too good for me… The story was full of action and, as 'Johnny Williams,' a newsreel cameraman, I got into fights, dodged bullets, crawled through swamps and played long love scenes with Gene Tierney. The last was pure pleasure, but the swamp crawling was a chore, especially the time they forgot to call *cut*. I had crawled about two hundred yards before I discovered the rest of the company had been dismissed and was halfway home."

George was a familiar figure on the Hollywood social scene, but he was still a "hick" at heart. It was known that he neither smoked nor drank, and that he actually preferred to be in bed by ten. Gossip columnists tied him to Ginger Rogers, but her late hours didn't agree with him. And for a brief time he was even engaged to Hedy Lamarr.

Still saddled with his Montana drawl, George claimed ownership to only three suits of clothes – all gray – and when friends chided him for his small, unimaginative wardrobe, he'd reply, "You ever have seven brothers?" And while he may have considered himself a hick, he spoke Russian and German, and spent most of his spare time on the movie sets reading O'Neill, Shaw, and Coward.

"Frugal" was another label attached to him. "I'm saving up to buy cows," he'd tell critics. At the time, he owned a 1,444 acre ranch in Montana and hoped to build it to a 5,000 acre spread, as he said, "before audiences get wise to me."

His taste in women: "I don't care what she is so long as she can laugh. I'm too serious."

Enter Dinah Shore. She also had firm ideas as to what she wanted in a mate: "Just a nice, ordinary fellow. No mental giant, but a fellow with a sense of humor and sincerity. Not a success as Hollywood knows success – measured in popularity or fabulous sums – but just an ordinary guy, the kind one meets every day."

It was a classic case of love at first sight between two attractive people who did not particularly enjoy the casual, superficial intimacies characteristic to many in the fun-loving world of entertainment. With Dinah, there were also her old psychological problems that called for a more meaningful relationship: "I suffered from a desperate desire to be loved and needed."

On one of their first dates, George and Dinah went ice-skating, and when he knelt down to help Dinah with her skates, George noticed the unusually high arch in her foot. "What happened here?" he asked. "You break your foot once?" All at once that old feeling of guilt that had been instilled in her from childhood seized her. She pulled the foot away and replied, "Yes, I broke it a long time ago."

A bit later, as they were skating around the rink, Dinah realized she should have told George the truth. "I lied when I told you I'd broken my foot," she told George. "When I was a child, I had polio. I didn't want you to know."

George couldn't help laughing. "That's the most ridiculous thing I've ever heard," he said. "What do you think we do with former cripples in Montana? Shoot them?"

He hugged her tightly, and they continued to glide about the rink. That was the last time Dinah ever felt self-conscious about her childhood affliction.

It wasn't long before the press began focusing attention on the attractive couple. "We're a fine pair," George told interviewers. "We go to a movie and along about nine o'clock my eyes start to burn with sleepiness, and I look over at Dinah and hers are beginning to droop. We're hard-working people and have no time for late parties or nightclubs. I love to go up to her home for dinner. The house is usually full of radio people, and Dinah is usually making the hot biscuits when I get there. It's just an easygoing good time and we like it."

Montgomery, who'd just completed work on *Bomber's Moon* at Fox, had recently joined the Army Signal Corps and now held the rank of corporal. Regrettably, he and Dinah had been seeing each other steadily for only a couple of weeks when he received word that – effective immediately – he was going to be stationed in Alaska. For the next few months, at least, their courtship would have to be continued via the mails.

George may have been absent, but Dinah's life was anything but idle. She had her two radio shows, recordings ("You'd Be So Nice to Come Home To") and there were movies to do. Her role in Samuel Goldwyn's *Up in Arms* gave her much more screen time than she'd had in *Thank Your Lucky Stars*. As an Army nurse, she was the female lead in this Technicolor piece of escapist fare, playing opposite comedian Danny Kaye, who was making his film debut after scoring a solid hit in Broadway's *Let's Face It*.

Elliot Nugent directed the February 1944 release about a hypochondriac draftee, which was based on Owen Davis' play *The Nervous Wreck*. Also in the cast were Dana Andrews, Constance Dowling, and Louis Calhern. Dinah said about the film, "In the cinematically arranged scuffle, I had my first chance to play screen comedy, plus an opportunity to sing two of my favorite numbers, 'Now I Know' and 'Tess' Torch Song.'...All this and Danny Kaye, too! Working with Danny was a party with pink icing, and our zoot-suit number was its high spot. I wore a sort of hussy dress for this dance number, velvet skirt, striped bodice and black lace stockings."

Dinah and Danny got along beautifully while filming *Up in Arms*, developing a lasting friendship. Clowning around, in fact, became their favorite pastime. One writer from *Photoplay* recalled a luncheon he attended with the pair on the Goldwyn lot, when both rose from the table and, "for the edification of the diners, went into the darndest routine you ever saw."

As a vehicle to introduce the deft talents of Mr. Kaye, *Up in Arms* was an unqualified success and received generally good notices from the nation's critics. Said the *Los Angeles Examiner*: "There are a million laughs, and while the comedy is whacky and must be accepted that way, it is done with taste, enhanced by Technicolor." And of Dinah, that paper commented: "How the boys in the service love that girl and how she can 'torch'. She is a fine foil for Kaye."

Follow the Boys from Universal was another of those all-star packages in which Dinah was one of a couple dozen stars who stuck her head "in the door," did her bit, then disappeared. Dealing with the Hollywood Victory Committee and the USO camp shows, this March 1944 release required Miss Shore to sing three tunes: "I'll Get By," "I'll Walk Alone," and "Mad About Him Blues." Among the other stars who appeared in the Eddie Sutherland-directed collage were George Raft, Orson Welles, Jeanette MacDonald, Marlene Dietrich, W.C. Fields, the Andrews Sisters and Donald O'Connor.

Reviews were mixed, with the *New York Times* observing "...as orderly screen composition, it hasn't the slightest claim."

Professionally, things couldn't really have been better for Dinah. Her 1942 earnings were estimated at about $115,000, and for two years running she was voted the top feminine singing star by the nation's radio editors, and the Fashion Academy named her the "Best Dressed Woman" in the field of supper clubs, one of many such honors she would receive in the course of her career. She was working hard in all the entertainment mediums and, on one occasion, became so exhausted that she even condescended once to try a drink. She recalled the incident in a 1943 interview: "One night after a broadcast, I was tired and someone said, 'What you need is a stingeroo.' So I drank one, and pretty soon I knocked a glass of water on the floor and I began to talk funny – and never, never, never again!"

What Dinah really wanted was for George to return. Near the end of 1943, he was back in Hollywood on one of his infrequent furloughs. It was then – thirteen months after their first meeting – that they decided to elope. At 2:30 Sunday morning, December 5, 1943, the couple was married by Justice of the Peace Paul O'Malley in Las Vegas. They were wed under their original names – George Letz and Frances Rose Shore – but the following October they appeared before a Los Angeles Superior Court judge and had their professional names made legal.

Immediately after the wedding ceremony, Dinah sent her sister Bessie a wire: "Just hitched up that third initial and can now monogram my linens." It was a private joke between the sisters. When Dinah was buying linens for her apartment, Bessie had kiddingly suggested she should have a third initial before she had them monogrammed.

"I'll never forget that when George and I were driving home from being married in Las Vegas, we heard a radio commentator say he gave our marriage three weeks," reflected Dinah in a 1954 interview. "The memory of that prediction has made me constantly on guard against cheating on my husband and children in favor of my career."

5.

The War Years

S<small>EPARATIONS WERE THE RULE, RATHER THAN THE EXCEPTION DURING THE</small> first couple of years of the Montgomery marriage. The United States was engaged in a world war, and Dinah and George, each in their own way, were doing their part to bring about the ultimate victory.

Dinah was among the most active of show business personalities who donated their time and talent to the war effort. Virtually the entire show business community did its part either on the home front or as members of the armed forces. Even before the bombing of Pearl Harbor, volunteer Robert Montgomery was in embattled France, driving an ambulance on the front lines, while actors like Jimmy Stewart – who left a $1500 per week job at Metro – and Douglas Fairbanks, Jr., had joined the military. Other performers, such as Dorothy Lamour, Merle Oberon, Madeline Carroll and Fred MacMurray took an active part in supporting Bundles for Britain, and Englishman Basil Rathbone headed the Hollywood chapter of British War Relief.

Once the Japanese had pulled off their surprise attack, even more Hollywood personalities became deeply involved in various home-front causes. With the West Coast in constant fear of attack, the plush Malibu beach-home area was fortified, and Cesar Romero, Buster Keaton and other personalities joined the Volunteer Evacuation Corps, whose purpose was to move civilians inland should there be an enemy landing.

As in World War I, stars volunteered to peddle war bonds. Personalities like James Cagney, Fred Astaire, Cary Grant, Dorothy Lamour, Al Jolson, Glenn Ford and the Marx Brothers toured the country in the war-bond campaign. Kate Smith alone, singing Irving Berlin's "God Bless America," sold one-hundred-eight million dollars worth in an eighteen-hour period.

Another method of reaching the public was through the camera itself. Loretta Young, Jane Withers, and others filmed short war-bond appeals, which were shown in theaters around the nation.

One of the traveling fund raisers was Hollywood's first war casualty. Lovely blonde Carole Lombard was killed in a January 1942 plane crash outside of Las Vegas while on the way home from a successful Indianapolis bond rally. Her husband, Clark Gable, totally distressed at his wife's untimely death, enlisted in the Army Air Corps, ultimately becoming a gunner on a bomber and rising to the rank of major. He was not the only star to forsake his career in favor of service to his country. Tyrone Power, Henry Fonda, Gene Kelly, Gene Autry, and Wayne Morris, who was to become a combat ace in the South Pacific, were just a few of the leading men who signed up.

Veronica Lake, in a sense, also made a supreme sacrifice. In the interest of safety, she did away with her peek-a-boo hairstyle, which had been adopted by women around the country. Government officials had feared such long tresses might be hazardous for female factory workers, in that they could become caught in high-speed machinery. One of the actress' stray curls, incidentally, was sold for one hundred eighty-six thousand dollars at a bond rally.

War songs of the forties were of a sentimental nature with tunes like "The Last Time I Saw Paris," "There'll Be Bluebirds Over the White Cliffs of Dover," "I Left My Heart at the Stage Door Canteen," and "God Bless America" getting much of the play.

Certainly the most memorable contribution celebrities made to the war effort was their total devotion to lifting the serviceman's morale – both at home and on the front lines. Many stars, for instance, opened their homes to the off-duty soldiers, inviting large groups over for dinner or Sunday brunch around the swimming pool. Jeannette MacDonald and her husband, Gene Raymond, were a couple who did this often.

Eddie Cantor created his Purple Heart Circuit, in which performers toured hospitals to entertain wounded soldiers. Dinah was a regular in this Cantor troupe. There was also the "Lunchtime Follies" – troupes of actors who provided noon shows for factory workers.

Less prominent actors were signed to appear – for a modest salary – in USO camp shows, which toured the various military bases around the country presenting everything from a ten-girl orchestra to legit productions of proven hits like *My Sister Eileen*, and a streamlined production of *Hamlet*, by Major Maurice Evans, which also played in the Pacific theater.

In both Hollywood and New York, show business personnel staffed Stage Canteens that catered to the serviceman on leave. On any given night, a soldier or sailor could go to one of these USO sponsored clubs and watch the biggest stars (Durante, Crosby, Cantor, etc.) perform; dance with the most beautiful starlets; and be waited upon by anyone from Hedy Lamarr to John Garfield to Bette Davis – all absolutely free. And, in the kitchen, luminaries like George Raft and Paul Henreid were kept busy washing dishes.

By the end of the war, over nine million free show tickets had been presented to servicemen, a truly magnanimous and costly gesture by the producers involved.

To further entertain the military man, Armed Forces Radio cut regular transcriptions, such as "Command Performance," featuring major stars like Bob Hope, Judy Garland, Groucho Marx and Lana Turner, to be played in both this country and abroad. Accommodating the soldiers as much as possible, hosting stars would read individual servicemen's letters over the air, then attempt to fulfill their requests by singing a particular song or bringing on a special guest star. Naturally, the Hollywood glamour girls – Betty Grable, Rita Hayworth, Lana Turner, Hedy Lamarr – were among those asked for most often.

It's said that the "Foxhole Circuit" – stretching through Europe and Northern Africa to the Wide Pacific and up to Alaska – was the biggest vaudeville chain in history. Virtually every performer of any stature made one or more trips to these theaters of conflict. One of the first to volunteer was Al Jolson, who worked so hard entertaining troops in Africa that he was hospitalized and forced to have a lung removed. Following his recovery, he spent much of his time playing bond rallies and hospitals.

Joe E. Brown was another tireless traveler. He had a special reason for committing himself to the servicemen; his son, Don, had been killed in a bomber crash. The wide-mouthed comedian told friends: "When you've lost your own boy, all other lads become your son." In 1945, Brown was presented with the Bronze Star for his continuing work in entertaining front-line troops in the Pacific.

"Personally, I never thought entertainment so damn important," reported Edgar Bergen, "but I changed my mind after we toured the army posts in Alaska." The experience was such a moving one for the ventriloquist, he claimed it took the fun out of performing for civilians.

Bing Crosby, Danny Kaye, John Wayne, Jack Benny, Marlene Dietrich (who opened a Canteen in Paris after the liberation), Edward G. Robinson, Humphrey Bogart, Yvonne DeCarlo, Ann Sheridan, Dick Powell, James Cagney, and Gary Cooper were just a few of the stars who went all over the globe to let our boys know that the people at home cared about what was happening to them. Those who couldn't sing, dance, or tell jokes, simply shook hands with the guys, ate with them, chatted awhile and, in the case of the ladies, gave out a lot of hugs and kisses.

It wasn't easy making those tours. The performers had to do several shows a day, sleep on planes or in jeeps and, perhaps most difficult, they had to maintain cheery smiles while walking through surgical and burn wards in field hospitals. But, troopers as they were, the show-biz folk pulled it off, bringing a little bit of happiness into the serviceman's miserable existence.

Surely no single performer traveled more to perform for servicemen during World War II or, for that matter, in any U.S. conflict since, than Bob Hope. Dubbed "Trader Corn" by the GI's, the comedian headed junket after junket, entertaining troops wherever he could find an audience – be it several thousand men or a mere dozen.

Dinah Shore's involvement in the war effort began soon after Pearl Harbor. She was the first radio star to sing for Selective Service inductees. In addition to her altruism, she had a personal reason for wanting to help lift the serviceman's morale. One of her former beaus after all, had been killed in that Sunday morning sneak-attack.

From the start of the conflict, Dinah was the military man's favorite songstress, and they proved the point by sending her approximately one thousand fan letters per week. She was even made an honorary member of the Seventh Regiment of the New York National Guard, the first woman to be so honored since Jenny Lind in 1852.

As far as the soldier and sailor were concerned, she was the *link* between themselves and their sweethearts at home. A favorite sentimental song, like "Stardust" or "I'm Dreaming of a White Christmas," sung by Dinah would be heard by both the serviceman and his girl, each aware that the other was listening, and bringing them together again – at least in spirit.

Request songs became a regular part of the singer's own radio programs as far back as 1942. On one broadcast, she sang "Russian Lullaby" for forty-one servicemen around the world and their girlfriends. "I know it sounds gushy," she explained, "but I cry when I read their letters. When a boy writes me that when I sang his girl's favorite song he shut his eyes and dreamed she was right beside him singin', I'm mighty happy all day, because I think maybe I helped him feel a little less lonely."

A virtual regular on Armed Forces Radio's "Command Performance," Dinah's distinct friendliness was responsible for her being requested to appear more often than any other star during the war years. The number of Armed Forces broadcasts that featured her (including shows like "Mail Call" and "Show Time") was well over one thousand.

Bob Hope tagged her "a juke box on a valentine," and Eddie Cantor said, "If it's a song, it's Dinah's kind of song." The guys who were far away from home agreed with the pros, whether they heard her sing on radio, records, at a hospital, training camp, or in a USO canteen. Warm, fresh, sweet Dinah – "Queen of the Jukeboxes" – was their kind of girl.

"There were times," she reflected, "when I was so bushed I could have gone home and stayed there for the duration. But no matter how tired I was, if I dragged myself out in front of a crowd of servicemen who really wanted to hear me and I started to sing, I wasn't tired anymore."

In the summer of 1942, Dinah was taking salt pills and touring the desert military camps outside of Los Angeles. With a piano on the back of a truck and often performing from a stage constructed of bales of hay, she sang to audiences as large as ten thousand – or as small as one. The latter performance took place at the Army Air-Gunnery School at Las Vegas, New Mexico. Departing the camp after singing for the trainees, she was hailed by the sentry, who called, "Goodnight, Miss Shore. Sorry I couldn't hear you tonight."

Dinah told her driver to stop and, from the auto's running board, sang the lonely sentry three of his favorite numbers.

Following a show for the Navy at San Francisco's Presidio one evening, an officer was escorting Dinah to her car when she noted that several sailors were wearing armbands marked "S.P."

"What does that mean?"

"Shore Patrol."

"My," she said with an innocent little smile, "that was very nice of you, but you shouldn't have gone to all that trouble."

Dinah had said "Goodnight" and was on her way back to her hotel before the flabbergasted officer realized she was pulling his leg.

Aside from putting in her time with the servicemen, Dinah also did her part in raising money for Defense Bonds. One rally at which she appeared took place in her hometown, Nashville, in March of 1942. They called it "Dinah Shore Day." Met at the train by her father, civic leaders and a cheering crowd, she was led through town by a motorcycle escort. The "local girl made good" was so moved by her reception that, on stage, she burst into tears and was unable to sing a note.

When Dinah and George Montgomery were married in December of 1943, he was unable to extend his furlough and she had professional commitments that prevented them from going on a honeymoon. The following July, however, they were able to break away and, with Ticker Freeman and his wife accompanying them, began the long drive to Montana, where George planned to introduce his new bride to his family, who now occupied a twenty-thousand-acre ranch.

"Dinah wanted to prove what a fine little housewife she could be," remembered Freeman. "She said she would do the cooking for the whole family when we reached George's home. George, with a straight face, agreed. Boy, was she surprised when she learned she had to cook for the four of us,

George's parents, his twelve brothers and sisters and various ranch hands – about thirty altogether."

Dinah has said of the experience, "By the time the dishes were washed, they came in for lunch, and when these were dried and stacked, they were back for dinner."

The singer certainly showed her in-laws that she was not a spoiled Hollywood girl, endearing herself to them by her extraordinary efforts in the kitchen. She even wound up spraining her ankle while – during a respite from her chores – she played softball with the family: "I think I really won them over when I sat down and ate fried rabbit, which I hated and they loved."

Once their vacation was over, the Montgomerys again answered their individual calls to duty. George was sent to a military base in Georgia and, when he later returned to the West Coast, stopped off briefly in Nashville to get acquainted with his wife's family.

"Mr. Shore had been very disappointed that Dinah had married outside her faith," reports a childhood friend of the singer. "He was, after all, an Orthodox Jew. But, I understand that, once he met George, he liked him and they got along quite well."

While her husband was away, Dinah completed her scenes on another movie, then left for Europe to begin an eight-week USO tour.

Arriving at Scotland's trans-Atlantic ATC air terminal during the first week in August, Dinah and her troupe of entertainers (pianist Ticker Freeman, a comedian, and a magician) made a whirlwind visit through the hospital wards, where wounded American soldiers were kept briefly before being flown back to the States. Veterans of the Normandy landing clamored for a song and she obliged with "Stardust" and "I Can't Give You Anything But Love." She autographed leg, arm, and body casts, and even became a patient herself when a medic re-bandaged the sprained ankle she'd sustained in her recent Montana softball game.

The ankle had been twisted again when an enterprising young photographer asked her to climb on a table and pose with her legs crossed. Wearing a USO blouse and slacks, Dinah quipped: "You can't get a cheesecake picture of a girl in slacks."

Five weeks after D-Day, Dinah Shore – attired in helmet, uniform, and men's shoes much too large for her – waded ashore on Omaha Beach and put on a short show twenty minutes later. "Several soldiers," she reported, "asked for my autograph before the show – 'Just because you're a girl.'

"I was no glamour portrait and when they looked at my signature they said, 'Quit kidding.'"

The entertainer played the French GI circuit from cow pastures to the Palace of Versailles (her biggest thrill), doing shows in a basement by candlelight, at Metz while a German plane was being shot down, and even atop an amphibious jeep.

"What impressed me the most," she reported, "was the amazing spirit of the French. Whenever some civilians attended the shows, I would ask them to come up on the stage and sing the 'Marseillaise' with me. There was something defiant in the way the grown-ups sang, but so sweet and hopeful when the children burst into their national anthem, which had been taught to them in whispers by fathers and mothers who never knew if a German would be listening outside their door."

One soldier she met in France was Pfc. Emmett R. Anderton, Jr., of Winchester, Tennessee, an old childhood playmate with whom she spent a couple of hours reminiscing. Later, Anderton wrote to Dinah's sister, Bessie Seligman, who was then living back in Nashville with her family, and reported, in part: "She is fine – working very hard – and on the go all the time from morning to night. You don't know how much we appreciate the great job she's doing for the boys. Most of her entertaining is being done right up close to the front and with boys who have been in the thick of it since D-Day.

"She is gathering up all kinds of souvenirs, gifts from high-ranking officers, and even has one of the largest captured German machine guns. She's also keeping that camera of hers busy taking the highlights of her trip."

Dinah and Ticker had completed one of their shows when they were invited into a tent for some refreshments and introduced to twenty-six officers. As they were leaving, the singer thanked the officers, addressing *each* by name and rank. "I was staggered," remembered Freeman a few years later, "and so were the officers. I've never seen such a fabulous memory. But then Dinah constantly amazes me."

Discussing the incident, Miss Shore chuckled: "What Ticker doesn't realize is that I did it to stagger him. It wasn't hard to remember the names – old campus politics, you know. People like to be remembered. But I have to throw Ticker once in a while or life would get pretty dull."

On another occasion, she was to be present at the dedication of a new military bridge – the "Dinah Shore Bridge." Suddenly, there was a shot and everybody dived for cover. Everybody except Dinah, that is. Spotting the German sniper, she calmly walked over and snapped his picture.

Entertaining the soldiers in France at the same time as Dinah was crooner Bing Crosby, and the two performers finally got together outside of Verdun. GI's on their way back from the front lines were pleasantly surprised to see Bing and Dinah walking toward them singing "It Ain't Necessarily So."

Whereas the boys were intrigued with the white pumps Dinah wore, they were also taken with an item of Crosby's attire – his neckties. "Hey, Bing," they'd say, "just let me feel it!"

Dinah had first met "the Groaner" shortly after she arrived in Hollywood. An avid fan, she would steal into his radio studio on the days of his broadcasts – just to watch him work: "I was afraid to meet him. I knew I'd swoon."

When they were finally introduced at the studio *he* said, "I like your singing and I've wanted to meet you." Unable to think of a reply, she rushed from the studio to get some fresh air.

A bit later, when she was able to relax in his presence, Dinah and Bing worked together several times – including a number of "Command Performance" broadcasts.

Crosby and Fred Astaire were on stage with Dinah when she did her show for over twelve thousand Allied soldiers in the gardens of Versailles.

Although she spent most of her time in France with enlisted men, even putting on a special performance for two soldiers who arrived late for the regular show, Dinah had the opportunity to meet with both Generals Omar Bradley and George Patton on her trip. Patton presented her with a pearl-handled pistol after she sang for his Third Army.

"He's a man completely without inhibitions," she said of the general. "He's adored by his men, and you can always find him as near the firing line as any of them. In fact, he makes a point of traveling in his jeep without even wearing goggles so his men will know that he's with them."

It wasn't easy living out there with the soldiers in the field. Most of all, Dinah missed sleeping on crisp white bed sheets. She didn't even have a sleeping bag until she finally scrounged around and found one for herself. Until then, she'd washed her face towel out in her helmet during the day, hoping it would be dry enough to utilize as a pillow when her group bivouacked at night.

By the middle of September, she reached liberated Paris, where she visited one of the world's most famous beauty parlors to get her hair washed. Regrettably, the hot water wasn't hot and there was no electricity to run the dryers, but the beauticians wrapped her hair up in a towel and let nature take its course.

Dinah got a kick out of the way the French had needled the Germans and gotten away with it. She didn't see a green dress, necktie, awning, or bottle of crème de menthe in all of Paris. There wasn't anything green in the city except the grass and the French couldn't change that: "They eliminated everything green they could because green was the color of the German uniforms.

"They also hid their best things. I went into a toy store and got some beautiful dolls, which had been buried in the cellar away from the Germans for four years."

Before she headed back to the States, Dinah returned to London and, at the request of American psychological-warfare experts, performed a half-hour broadcast aimed at the retreating German soldier.

She began with a little speech, written phonetically in German: "German soldiers! Here talks Dinah Shore. I have just returned from Paris, where I sang for American troops. Meanwhile, our boys have entered Germany to re-establish order, freedom, and justice. I hope they will succeed soon, for then you will be able to return to your Fatherland and your families and start a new life."

Then she sang, starting with "I'll Get By," but substituting lyrics that said the Americans would get by the Siegfried and other German lines. Next, referring to Patton's men, she offered "Tanks a Million." She said something about the Atlantic Wall and then insinuatingly sang, "Long Ago and Far Away." Finally, there was "I'll Be Seeing You," unmistakably referring to no other place but Berlin.

Exhausted, but fulfilled from her arduous trip, Dinah was back home at the end of September. With the war in Europe going well for the Allies, it was time for life to, hopefully, drift back to normal. She and George had recently purchased a home in Beverly Hills and, after what she'd accomplished, the lady had earned the right to enjoy it.

In a 1955 interview with *Cue*, she attempted to explain the reasons for her tireless war work by declaring that she never felt she had anything resembling a great singing voice: "This is no line. I don't see why I've been successful. I think I sort of feel guilty about it. That may explain in part why I did so much entertaining of troops during the war. It was as if I were paying a debt."

Whatever her motivation, the USO appreciated her efforts and, in 1958, presented her with their fourth annual Medallion Award at a luncheon in the Beverly Hills Hotel. This was the first time in the organization's history that its annual award had been given to only one person.

She may not have fired any guns in the war, nor did she build any armaments, but by using her God-given talents to help raise the morale of those who were carrying out those tasks, Dinah had performed an invaluable service for her country.

6.

Radio, Records and Marriage

In a sense, George became a regular on Eddie Cantor's radio show soon after his marriage to Dinah – if not in-person, then by constant reference in the scripts. The "Montgomery gag," for instance, was used on one program that featured Cesar Romero as its guest. The sketch had the dashing screen "wolf" making a pass at Dinah, who retorts with, "Would you mind backing up a little. Your fangs are chipping the table."

Undaunted, Romero begins to kiss her hand – an act to which Dinah does not seem to object. As she explains to a bewildered Cantor: "His mustache gives my ring a nice polish."

Cesar, finally, backed off, but only after the songstress informed him he can call her by her "pet name": Mrs. George Montgomery.

When Montgomery himself guested on a show, the sketch had Dinah forcing him to go to one of Cantor's parties. The gag, of course, was that George considered Eddie to be a bore. Eager to seize any excuse to duck the affair Montgomery informs Dinah that he can't find his cuff links, to which she replies: "Why don't you look in the dresser?"

"If I do, I'm a dead pigeon."

Eddie remained the butt of the jokes when Dinah asks George: "Why do you look so unusually handsome to me tonight?"

"Because you've been looking at Cantor all day."

Milking this same line of humor, George queries Dinah: "Do I look anything like Eddie Cantor?"

She replies: "I married you, didn't I? Does that answer your question?"

Dinah and Cantor parted company in 1944. It was a pleasant separation, one that the comedian knew from the start was inevitable. She had simply become too busy to appear regularly on any program but her own. "Dad didn't want to hold onto Dinah after she was ready to go off to more important things," recalled Natalie Cantor, who married French actor Robert Clary.

Cantor remained a close friend of his former protégée and, in 1954 commented: "Like all the best people in show business, it is true of her that the bigger she gets, the nicer she becomes."

***

Any serious dreams Dinah had about a major career in motion pictures were not encouraged by the January 1945 release of *Belle of the Yukon*, the film she'd completed just prior to her European jaunt. Headlining the *Belle* cast were Randolph Scott, Gypsy Rose Lee, Charles Winninger, and Bob Burns, with William Marshall playing Dinah's romantic interest. William A. Seiter directed from James Edward Grant's screenplay. It opened to mixed reviews and was typical of the saccharine type of movies she was to be offered from that time forward.

"The story line of every script sent to me was like the one in my picture, *Belle of the Yukon*," she said to the *Saturday Evening Post* in 1959. "In it, I played a pure-as-untracked-snow girl whose father ran a gambling house. I fell in love with a fellow who was suspected of being something other than he was; it doesn't matter now what. That was merely part of what was known as 'the complications.' I can sum the plot up in five sentences: Girl sings to boy. Girl suspects boy is not what he's supposed to be. Boy leaves. Girl sings about boy. Boy comes back, and they live happily ever after because girl was wrong about boy; he was what he was supposed to be all the time.

"I didn't regenerate him because that would have required acting somewhat beyond my capabilities."

In discussing her contribution to the Technicolor RKO release, the *Los Angeles Examiner* said, "Dinah Shore, most unflatteringly photographed, sings like an angel – nothing else but an angel."

On a more positive note, Dinah continued to hold her high position on the record charts during 1945. Her two hit discs for Victor were "Dandy" and "Along the Navajo Trail."

Yet, perhaps more important than her career these days was the fact that George's military duties were allowing him to be at home more often than not. It was a welcome change from their first year or so of marriage, which had seen Montgomery stationed in San Antonio, Texas, for much of the time. Now, at least, the couple could really start to get acquainted and disprove the upsetting rumors that the marriage was on the verge of collapse. "I often cried myself to sleep," Dinah recalled, "I wanted the world to know that I loved him and he loved me."

Married life agreed with Dinah, giving her the stability she'd always wanted: "Before I met George, my life was an omelet: everything was mixed up from day to day; nothing was planned. I used to go around in sloppy sweaters, droopy skirts, and scuffed shoes. But after I was married, I began to see that I couldn't live from one second to the next and be happy.

"It's a matter of knowing when to save and when to spend it. George taught me that I'd been burning myself out with all those senseless activities; I really think I'd have been finished in a year or two if I hadn't had enough sense to hook George."

The singer and her husband were back in Nashville in April to visit her sixty-six-year-old father, who had undergone major surgery at Vanderbilt University Hospital. Ginny Sims replaced Dinah on her radio show during her brief absence.

"George was so good to Solomon," remembered a family member. "He even shaved him in his hospital bed."

Solomon Shore was reported as "improving rapidly," so, while they were in town, Dinah and George entertained at a special Red Cross benefit presented at Thayer Hospital, then returned to Los Angeles.

The elder Shore died a month later. Dinah arrived in Nashville several hours after his passing at the hospital, remaining until sometime following his burial at the K.K.A.L. Cemetery. It was, understandably, a trying time for the entire Shore-Montgomery-Seligman clan.

Shortly after Solomon's death, the Montgomerys decided to get away for a while and took a needed vacation back at the family ranch in Montana. "We'll probably do a little fishing," she informed the press prior to their departure.

***

The prime activity on Dinah's full schedule now was her popular half-hour radio show, sponsored by Bird's-Eye frozen foods every Thursday night at 8:30 over NBC. She retained Harry von Zell as her announcer, but there was a new facet on this program. Appearing as a regular guest was Groucho Marx.

"Groucho wasn't easy for her to work with," reflects Walter Bunker, producer-director of the entertainment. "He was too zany and ad-libbed too much."

Dinah was truly out-classed by the comedian's sharp wit and, at times, didn't seem to know how to deal with his impromptu remarks. Conversely, Groucho, saddled with lines and sketches inferior to his own deft off-hand remarks, was not at his best either. Marx was with the show for a total of twenty-six weeks.

For the 1946-47 season, Ford Motor company bought Dinah's program, switching the entertainment to Wednesday nights and putting it on CBS. Although she'd still sing five tunes per program to the music of Robert Emmett Dolan's orchestra, the format on this new entry was revamped to emphasize less nonsensical comedy. Peter Lind Hayes was signed as a regular.

When they got around to analyzing that season in June of 1947, Dinah and her advisors decided she had better stick to *singing* on the radio, and leave the comedy to experienced comediennes. It wasn't that she performed so badly in this new area, but then, why should Joe DiMaggio play football?

After *Belle of the Yukon*, Dinah was still being sought for films, however no longer was she asked to act – merely sing. Metro-Goldwyn-Mayer signed her to warble two songs (supposedly as Broadway star Julia Sanderson) in their Technicolor musical, *Till the Clouds Roll By*, which purported to tell the life of composer Jerome Kern. Released at the end of 1946, this loosely-structured but entertaining Arthur Freed production had its greatest strength in a series of lavishly-staged musical numbers performed by the MGM roster of players: June Allyson performed the title tune with Ray McDonald, then did "Cleopatterer" alone; Judy Garland (as Marilyn Miller) sang "Who" and "Look for the Silver Lining"; Van Johnson and Lucille Bremer were lively with "I Won't Dance; and the likes of Frank Sinatra, Angela Lansbury, Gower Champion, and Cyd Charisse rendered other Kern classics. One interesting innovation was the movie's opening, featuring Kathryn Grayson, Tony Martin, Lena Horne, Virginia O'Brien, and Caleb Peterson in a seventeen-minute condensed version of the composer's greatest success, *Show Boat*. Richard Whorf directed the dramatic sections of the movie, which had Robert Walker as Kern, Dorothy Patrick as his wife, and Van Heflin playing his arranger. Robert Alton staged the musical sequences, except for the two featuring Miss Garland. Vincente Minnelli, the star's husband, did those.

Variety: "Dinah Shore does an exceptional singing job on "They Didn't Believe Me," but didn't spark "The Last Time I Saw Paris" quite so effectively."

Visually, she was off the screen altogether in two animated cartoon features from Walt Disney Productions, which only made use of her voice. *Make Mine Music* (1946) was a charming series of cartoon interludes set, for the most part, to popular music performed by the likes of Dinah, Benny Goodman, Nelson Eddy, Jerry Colonna, the Andrews Sisters and Andy Russell. Among the more notable segments were "The Whale Who Wanted to Sing at the Met," "Johnny Fedora and Alice bluebonnet," "Peter and the Wolf," "All the Cats Join In" and "Casey at the Bat."

The *Los Angeles Times*: "The combination of Dinah Shore with her singing and Riabouchinska and Lichine [of the Ballet Russe] as dancing partners approached sheer perfection in 'Two Silhouettes,' which will probably be the most happily remembered of the beautiful elements in Disney's fantasy."

In *Fun and Fancy Free* (1947), which *Newsweek* claimed was made by "an uninspired Disney working on a strictly commercial basis," Dinah narrated *Bongo*, the first of two short stories that made up the seventy-three minute film. She also sang two numbers ("Lazy Countryside" and "Say It with a Slap") in this tale of a talented, undersized circus bear who yearns to escape his confines for the freedom of the forest.

For the second-half of the movie, Edgar Bergen, Charlie McCarthy and Mortimer Snerd served as hosts in an adaptation of *Jack and the Beanstalk*, featuring Mickey Mouse, Donald Duck, and Goofy.

Dinah's filmic fortunes, momentarily, seemed to take a turn for the better near the end of the decade when MGM's Dore Schary approached her and suggested that she play the tragic "Julie" in the studio's upcoming remake of *Show Boat* (1951), which would star Howard Keel and Kathryn Grayson. "I was thrilled," she remembered. "I tested for it and they told me my test was good, but in the end they cast somebody in it who was much better."

What had actually happened is that studio executive Schary had talked to Dinah about the role without checking first with Arthur Freed, the project's producer. Though Freed liked Dinah and admired her singing talent, he didn't think she was right for this particular part. Ultimately, he got Schary off the hook by convincing the lady that it would be damaging to her public image if she played "a whore," which is what the character wound up as at the end of the story.

Sultry Ava Gardner got the assignment and, according to a very gracious Miss Shore, "there couldn't have been a more perfect or exquisite Julie."

There was talk that Dinah would co-star with Betty Hutton in a film dealing with the lives of the Duncan sisters. That picture never came about, but she did do another movie – her last except for later cameo bits as herself in *Oh, God!* with George Burns (1977) and Robert Altman's *HealtH* (1980).

Aaron Slick from Punkin Crick was an ancient play by Walter Benjamin Hare, which Paramount executive Y. Frank Freeman had wanted to film for years. He had a nostalgic feeling about the old chestnut, since it had been his high school play. Sadly, his dream finally became a reality.

"My only regret is that we made the picture at all," claimed Claude Binyon, who both directed and wrote the screenplay for the 1952 Technicolor adaptation. The melodrama cast Dinah as a sweet innocent farm girl, pursued by both hero Alan Young and dastardly villain Robert Merrill. Describing Dinah's contribution to the dull effort, the *Hollywood Reporter* said: "Dinah Shore is charming as the girl and puts life and vitality into the songs."

Hollywood columnist James Bacon, who was then writing for *Associated Press*, recalls that when the picture was released, a Paramount publicist arranged for him to interview Dinah: "We drove out to the Montgomery house and were greeted by George. He explained that Dinah wasn't there.

To pass some time, he gave us a tour of the place, then after admitting that his wife had deliberately 'ducked' me because she was too embarrassed to talk about this terrible film, we proceeded to discuss his hobby of making furniture. This became the basis for my story. I really felt sorry for the poor press agent. When we were driving back to the studio, he asked: 'Can you at least say he makes furniture with an "Aaron Slick" finish?'"

"I bombed as a movie star," Dinah frankly admitted. "I failed for a lot of reasons. The most important was I'm not particularly photogenic...Also, every motion picture I've been in was tailored for somebody else, then they threw in a part for a girl singer."

Had Dinah been fortunate enough to have been signed by a major studio, she might have fared better on the screen. Certainly such an arrangement worked well for Doris Day, who was under contract to Warner Brothers from 1948 until the mid-fifties. With a financial stake in Miss Day that extended beyond a single picture, the studio saw to it that she was stunningly photographed and that specific properties were developed with her in mind.

Montgomery's post-war movies were nothing to get excited about either. Returning to Fox after his discharge to finish out his contract, the actor found his competition for choice assignments much stiffer than when he'd left. Tyrone Power and other top-flight leading men were back in civilian clothes also, a situation which relegated George to an artistically frustrating series of movies, which kept him working but failed to bolster his career. Among the less forgettable productions were *Three Little Girls in Blue* (1946) with June Haver; *The Brasher Doubloon* (1947), a bland Philip Marlowe mystery; *Belle Starr's Daughter* (1948) starring Ruth Roman; and, on loan-out to Columbia, *Lulu Belle* (1948) with Dorothy Lamour.

Away from the studios, George was developing a hobby that would eventually turn into a paying proposition. As a boy on his father's ranch in Montana, he'd been a constant whittler. Every piece of firewood that came his way was carved into some object. Once he departed for Los Angeles, however, the performer dropped his pastime – until two years or so after he and Dinah were married.

The couple purchased a large ranch, complete with chickens, in the San Fernando Valley, and under George's direction the house was remodeled to suit their tastes. But when it came to furnishing the place, they were stumped, unsure whether they should purchase costly antiques and reproductions in order to find something that would come close to expressing their informal way of life.

Dinah suggested that George design a few pieces of furniture, which he did and when both decided that they liked his ideas, he began to build the pieces himself. "I've not only made every stick in our house," he said in 1949, "but any number of pieces for our friends as well – mostly traditional, but some modern." These friends included such notables as Alan Ladd, Joel McCrea, Dorothy Lamour and Jeanne Crain.

His creations were so popular that he hired six cabinet makers and opened up his own furniture shop, turning it into a profitable business, which didn't interfere with his movie work.

Dinah and George enjoyed entertaining and often had other show-business couples over to their home, which they tagged "the house that George built." One evening, for example, the Dick Powells (June Allyson) and the Tony Bartleys (Deborah Kerr) might come by for what Dinah called a "name your own dish" dinner (i.e. the first invited guest plans the menu and Dinah prepares it herself – without the aid of hired help.) Afterwards, the group would sit around and be led in a sing-a-long by Miss Shore, accompanied by the guitar.

May of 1947 was a wonderful month for the Montgomerys, for that's when Dinah informed her husband, and the world, that she was going to have a baby. "We are thrilled to death," she told reporters, and answered the usual gender-preference question with, "We want both a boy *and* a girl."

Seven-pound Melissa Ann Montgomery entered the world via cesarean at Cedars of Lebanon Hospital in Los Angeles on January 4, 1948. "All three of us doing fine," George wired the *Nashville Banner*.

Shortly after Melissa's arrival, the lie that had circulated at the beginning of the decade surfaced again. "Dinah Shore has given birth to a black baby!" is what the muckrakers whispered. Like its predecessor, this tale had absolutely no basis in truth either; yet, it too has been kept alive by malicious backyard gossips.

Being a mother, Dinah began to take stock of herself and gave serious thought to retiring: "I just didn't feel like going back to work. I wanted to be with my baby," she said. But, quitting was not for her. She missed show business and, furthermore, infant Melissa slept most of the day anyway. Truly, how could she stop when her career – except the movie aspects – was going so well? It was an important decision for her to make – one that would have strong residual effects years later.

Back in 1946, Dinah had switched her record-company affiliation from Victor-Bluebird to Columbia. The move had been a wise one, for it put her recording career under the expert guidance of company vice president Manie Sacks who, years before as a Victor executive, had suggested to Xavier Cugat that he use Dinah for the Latin album that featured "The Thrill of a New Romance."

At Columbia, Dinah turned out one hit after another, seventy percent of which were ballads. "Shoo Fly Pie," a novelty number, sold four-hundred thousand discs, while "The Gypsy." "Doin' What Comes Natur'lly," and "For Sentimental Reasons" attracted a million buyers each. Indeed, *Billboard* magazine's 1946 Music-Record Poll listed Dinah first in three categories: Top Female Vocalist on Disc Jockey Shows; Top-Selling Female Vocalist over Record Counters, and Top Female Vocalist on the Nation's Juke Boxes.

The run of good luck continued for her over the next several years. She had another million seller with "The Anniversary Song," giving Al Jolson's Decca rendition a run for its money, and also mined gold with tunes like "I Wish I Didn't Love You So," "Buttons and Bows" (two million copies sold), "Lavender Blue," "Far Away Places," "Baby, It's Cold Outside," and "Dear Hearts and Gentle People."

"Dear Hearts," incidentally, was recorded by Miss Shore as a thank-you to the people of Nashville who would always give her a warm welcome when she came home for a visit.

Sammy Fain, who composed the tune with Bob Hilliard, said, "I made a demo of the song and sent it to Dinah. She liked it, but sent back a request that we insert some reference to 'Tennessee' in the lyric. We agreed, and that's how her recording came about."

Like any top vocalist, one of Dinah's biggest headaches was the constant pressure from aspiring song writers to sing their untested numbers on radio or records. She would receive an average of three thousand requests per year to "try out" somebody's "masterpiece," be it from her laundress, or from her service-station attendant. "You come to expect it from nearly everyone," she told an interviewer in 1949, "but the other day I really had a shock. George and I have periodic health check-ups – metabolism, etc. – and the doctor came out to put us through the tests. He had finished and was fumbling with his equipment. I recall I was wondering why he didn't leave, when all of a sudden he mumbled: 'You know, I hate to say this, but I've written a song and I was wondering...'"

Winchester, Tennessee, declared "Dinah Shore Day" when the songstress returned to her home town in 1949 to visit old friends at the annual Franklin County Fair. She sang "You Made Me Love You" to the hundreds of people who gathered to see the once little crippled girl who lived on 2nd Avenue. Many in the crowd recalled the times Dinah sang from the counter of her father's store. And when she was made an honorary Tennessee colonel at the occasion, Dinah couldn't help but comment, "You can't know how much this means to me. You see, George was only a corporal."

In September of that year, Dinah received another in her growing list of honors. She was named by the Southern California Fashion Institute to head the list of the "ten best-dressed women" in the United States, "because," according to the Institute representatives, "more than any other woman, she dresses to fit her type and the occasion." Among the others honored that year were Mary Livingston (Mrs. Jack Benny), Loretta Young, Mrs. Louis B. Mayer and Mrs. Jules Stein, wife of the board chairman of MCA.

Aside from her records and now thrice-weekly radio program, which she now did with Jack Smith and Margaret Whiting for Oxydol, Dinah was spending much of her time doing nightclub work and other personal appearances. She sang at the Shamrock Hotel in Houston; Los Angeles' fabulous Coconut Grove, where she was introduced opening night by Jack Benny, who didn't charge a cent; and at the Waldorf Astoria in New York. That engagement brought her a brutal review in the *New Yorker* from a critic who "found her singing a bit monotonous," and claimed that she had "a slim talent for putting over a song."

Dinah was a favorite of President Harry Truman and had entertained the Chief Executive at the White House and again by special invitation when he visited Los Angeles to be honored at a luncheon in the Coconut Grove. She and comedian Red Skelton were the only two performers who appeared at that West Coast affair, which was sponsored by the Los Angeles Press Club. Once she'd sung, "You Made Me Love You," Dinah asked the President if he would like to hear "Nature Boy," to which he replied with an emphatic

"Yes." The Trumans – including daughter Margaret – vigorously applauded the afternoon performance.

Despite the President's being a loyal fan of hers, Dinah was more than willing to oppose Truman anytime she disagreed with his actions. When, in 1950, he ordered paraplegic and tubercular war veterans transferred from a San Fernando Valley hospital to one in Long Beach, she got after celebrities like Bob Hope, Jack Benny, Fibber McGee and Molly, and Frances Langford to bombard the President with protests, and even used part of her radio show to tell how disabled homeowners would lose all their savings by the move: "Their houses are built around them and their wheelchairs. They've got special doors and plumbing nobody else would need. They're practically worthless on the current market.

"Morale is the important thing in the rehabilitation of these boys. Right now they're all wa-a-ay down in the dumps. One doctor told me the move might be fatal to some of the tubercular patients."

Dinah was a nice, soft-spoken lady, but when she had something to say, she said it!

***

Miss Shore had had a huge success at the London Palladium when she played there during the summer of 1948. She was invited back in late 1950 to appear with Jack Benny in the Royal Variety Show, attended by King George VI, and the Princesses Elizabeth and Margaret. "I was so excited, I was almost stricken," mused Dinah about her introduction to the royal family. "When Queen Elizabeth came down the receiving line, I reached out and grabbed her hand and shook like mad. When I was in school I dreamed about things like this…But never in my wildest fantasies did I think I'd be singing for a real king and queen."

In the early fifties, Dinah made her initial appearances with symphony orchestras, although Philadelphia conductor Alexander Smallens certainly disapproved of the idea of a popular singer "fronting" *his* seventy-piece orchestra. Set to croon "It's De Lovely" and "I Didn't Know What Time It Was," at the Philadelphia concert hall, Dinah sent Ticker Freeman on ahead to confer with Smallens regarding her arrangements. According to newspaper reports, when informed of the plan, the classical conductor hurled the popular music from him and stalked out of the rehearsal.

Dinah, in spite of the musician's ill feelings, kept her engagement.

Through her phenomenal success in motion pictures, Doris Day was, by 1951, giving Dinah some real competition for that coveted title of "top female vocalist." While the Gallup Poll named Miss Shore to that honor in January, many wags were saying that it would only be a matter of time before Doris, whose fans could *see* her regularly at their local movie house, would get the crown. But, this was the year that Dinah would enter an entirely new field of endeavor, one which would bring her into people's homes and, ultimately, make her one of the most popular female stars of the decade.

Fanny Rose Shore (seated center) at her 4th birthday party.
Standing behind the future Dinah Shore is her sister, Bessie.
(Photo courtesy of the Goldring/Woldenberg Institute of Southern Jewish Life.)

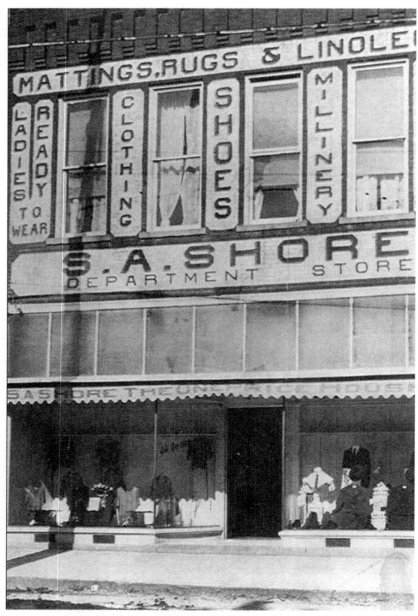

Solomon Shore's Department Store in Winchester, TN.
(Photo courtesy of the Goldring/Woldenberg Institute of Southern Jewish Life.)

Dinah with comedian Eddie Cantor in publicity shot for his NBC radio show.

Dinah appeared with Dana Andrews and Danny Kaye in the Technicolor musical,
Up in Arms, for Samuel Goldwyn.

Dinah rehearses with Frank Sinatra and Bing Crosby for an Armed Forces Radio
show. That's Ticker Freeman at the piano.

Dinah played "Julia Sanderson" in MGM's *'Till the Clouds Roll By.*

Mr. And Mrs. George Montgomery with daughter Melissa, either arriving
or departing from somewhere via train.

Dinah charms Alan Young in this publicity shot from Aaron Slick from *Punkin Crick* (1952), a film she wanted to forget.

Dinah wins an Emmy.

George and Dinah at a 1958 Hollywood premiere.

George and Dinah chat with President John F. Kennedy at the 1961 Radio
and Television Correspondents dinner.
(Photo courtesy of the John F. Kennedy Presidential Library and Museum.)

Dinah joined comedian Jack Benny on more than one of his television specials.

On one episode of *Dinah's Place*, the theme was "The Oscars."

Just Dinah.

Singer Robert Goulet, a guest on *Dinah!*, sips a variety of liquors, as he tells his hostess about the various countries he has visited. *(That must have been a fun show.)*

In this segment of *Dinah!*, Miss Shore sings and dances with Don Chrichton, lead dancer on *The Carol Burnett Show*.

When Sammy Davis, Jr. guested on *Dinah!*, the hostess held Sammy's cue cards
while he delivered a song.

Comedian Ronnie Schell, singers Rosemary Clooney, Gordon MacRae
and Shirley Jones visit with Miss Shore on an episode of *Dinah!*

Robert Wagner was a surprise guest on *Dinah!* when the show honored legendary actress Bette Davis.

Michael Caine and Sean Connery joined Dinah for a chat on her afternoon show.

When *Dinah!* aired some shows from Australia, singer Diana Trask did an Aussie
number with Dinah.

Dinah and boy friend Burt Reynolds attend a Hollywood party.

Dinah swings her club at her Colgate-Dinah Shore Winners Circle Golf
Championship tournament.

A thoughtful moment.

7.

Early TV

TELEVISION, THAT ELECTRONIC MASS OF MACHINERY THAT ENABLED Dinah to be viewed by millions, contrary to popular belief, has been with us since the 1920's. A Schenectady station, General Electric's WGY, began broadcasting three days per week in 1928 with shows that included "The Queen's Messenger," a one-act spy melodrama. Then, two years later, NBC opened an experimental transmitter in New York City. At the end of the thirties, RCA was marketing its first sets to the public and, among the special events that had been televised by this time were the opening of the New York World's Fair; a production of *Susan and God*, starring Gertrude Lawrence; and a Princeton-Columbia baseball game, television's first sportscast.

Fred Waring, with his Pennsylvanians, was one of the first personalities to be seen on the new medium's micro-sized screens, and following this broadcast, he commented: "There is nothing new about television showmanship. It's just the same old showmanship in a new setting."

Commercial telecasting began in July of 1941 with a Dodgers-Pirates game from Ebbets Field over station WNBT. The face of a Bulova clock carried the advertising message. Some of the other programs aired that day were a Lowell Thomas newscast (sponsored by Sun Oil Company), a USO show, a video version of the popular radio quiz "Uncle Jim's Question Bee," and a simulcast edition of "Truth or Consequences."

The coming of World War II ostensibly put a freeze on television experimentation; however, vast wartime progress in the field of radar was ultimately applied to the broadcast industry, setting the stage for the first regularly scheduled television programs, which debuted via the coaxial cable in 1947. Approximately fourteen thousand American homes had postcard-sized screens then, and the lucky owners delighted in viewing such early creative efforts as "Howdy Doody," "Kukla, Fran and Ollie," "Leave It to the Girls," "Meet the Press," "Juvenile Jury," and "Kraft Television Theatre," as well as news making events like President Truman's State of the Union message and the World Series.

A year later, shows like "The Lone Ranger," "Philco Playhouse," Ted Mack's "Original Amateur Hour," "The Voice of Firestone," and a syndication of the old "Hopalong Cassidy" motion picture series hit the tube, but of greater significance, three of television's most viable personalities made their first appearances in 1948. Grimacing newspaper columnist Ed Sullivan began his twenty-three year run as the host of the spectacular variety entry, "Toast of the Town" (later tagged "The Ed Sullivan Show"); ukulele-strumming former disc jockey Arthur Godfrey endeared himself to viewers – first with "Talent Scouts," then on "Arthur Godfrey and His Friends" (1949); and "Uncle Miltie" became the hottest performer in show business.

Known as "Mr. Television," Milton Berle was the first major entertainer to appear in the new medium on a regular basis. His raucous hour-long weekly variety show, "The Texaco Star Theater," held the American public so tightly that it was almost impossible to lure a set owner out of his house on a Tuesday night. Indeed, Berle was probably responsible for the purchase of more television receivers than any other performer (one hundred ninety thousand were in use by the end of 1948), and made the networks aware that "star power" was the key to success in this new entertainment form.

In 1949 and 1950, a fresh crop of shows and personalities appeared in the network's never-ending battle to lure video viewers to their respective channels. Among the more memorable of the pioneering efforts were "The Goldbergs," starting Gertrude Berg; "Captain Video"; "The Big Story"; "The Colgate comedy Hour," with Dean Martin and Jerry Lewis; Eddie Cantor; Abbott and Costello; Jimmy Durante; "Your Show of Shows," featuring Sid Caesar and Imogene Coca; "What's My Line"; "Robert Montgomery Presents"; "Superman"; and "The Arthur Murray Dance Party."

And what was television's contribution to our culture? There were a number of differing opinions. Bing Crosby commented: "Well, I'd say it's pretty good, considering it's for nothing."

Said T.S. Eliot: "It's a medium of entertainment which permits millions of people to listen to the same joke at the same time, yet remain lonesome."

Fred Allen: "Television is a triumph of equipment over people, and the minds that control it are so small that you could put them in the navel of a flea and still have enough room beside them for a network vice-president's heart."

During the first few years of regular programming, networks made it a point to sign their most popular stars to long-term, non-option employment contracts. Executives who recalled the big radio talent raid staged by CBS against NBC back in the forties made these costly commitments. In one swift move, CBS "stole" Amos 'n' Andy, Jack Benny, and Edgar Bergen, leaving the competing network brass with their mouths agape. Thus, when television came along, it was deemed advisable by network executives, such as Sylvester "Pat" Weaver of NBC, to protect their valuable assets from a similar fate. Milton Berle was given a thirty-year deal, while others, like Jackie Gleason, Martha Raye, Eddie Fisher, and Jimmy Durante, signed agreements ranging from fifteen to twenty years.

What the decision-makers didn't know or realize at the time was that on television, a performer – with few exceptions – would wear out his welcome with the public much quicker than he would have on radio. This was particularly true of comedians, whose individual styles became all too familiar to their fans after a few years on the air. In their particular heydays, Milton Berle, Jackie Gleason, Sid Caesar and Imogene Coca, George Gobel, and Steve Allen topped the Neilsen ratings, but once the public tired of them, they disappeared from home screens. Unfortunately for the networks, many of these stars still had valid employment agreements, which they continued to collect on for many years after they were off the air.

Singers, in general, did not fare well on "the box" either. Kate Smith, Tennessee Ernie Ford, Eddie Fisher, Judy Garland, and even Frank Sinatra all had *limited* series runs, achieving varying degrees of video success.

It has been the "personalities" – those performers who kept their own talents at low profile while spotlighting the personalities and talents of others – who have captured the longevity records. Certainly names like Ed Sullivan, Arthur Godfrey, Arlene Francis, Garry Moore, Art Linkletter, Johnny Carson and Merv Griffin stand as substantial testimony to this thesis.

Of the comedians, only the late Jack Benny and Lucille Ball could point to extraordinary endurance records on television. And as far as the singers are concerned, one can acknowledge both Perry Como and Dean Martin when it comes to the men, but on the distaff side *nobody* can match the video run of Dinah Shore.

The trend in the early fifties was toward sticking top recording artists – like Perry Como – into their own fifteen-minute musical programs, which would be telecast by a network two or three times per week. Since Dinah was the country's most popular songstress, she was also sought after to headline such an entry. She was no stranger to television when she first joined the medium on a regular basis in 1951. Already there had been guest appearances on programs like Milton Berle's "Texaco Star Theater," and as far back as mid-1948, her agents had tried to sell both her and George in a situation-formatted television show.

After hearing strong arguments in favor of the move from Henry Jaffe, Dinah signed with NBC to do two live quarter-hour shows each week – Tuesdays and Thursdays at 7:30 pm. Set to sponsor was Chevrolet, hence beginning one of the longest advertiser-star relationships in the history of video.

Dinah's television appearance, incidentally, had no appreciable effect on her radio activity, since she continued doing her CBS entertainment with Jack Smith (and now Ginny Sims) every Monday, Wednesday, and Friday evenings.

Why was she maintaining such an arduous schedule? More than a few members of the press asked her that question, to which Dinah answered, "Because I love it and they're paying me to enjoy myself."

"The Dinah Shore Show" was an immediate hit, with critics calling it one of the few *inventive* song sessions on television. Much credit for the success belonged to the show's writer-producer-director, a forty-year-old former actor named Alan Handley, who described his star as "a rare combination of talent, beauty, brains, and sheer graciousness." Months earlier it had been Handley who'd devised the original format for Dinah's program, then accompanied NBC vice-president Fred Wile from New York to the Montgomery's Montana ranch to convince the lady she should try television in the first place.

Preparations for the first "Dinah Shore Show" went smoothly until three days before air time, when the star decided that instead of singing "I'll Be Seeing You" on the opener, she'd prefer to do the more catchy "Shrimp Boats." Handley tried to convince her that there was no time to make the change, since it would require a different dance routine that had been choreographed, as well as another setting (a Louisiana bayou instead of a penthouse terrace). Besides, this was the beginning of the weekend, and rounding up singers, dancers, and crew members wouldn't be easy.

Dinah appealed to Fred Wile, who phoned the producer from New York and told him to "Work it out," which, with considerable difficulty, he did. "I think in our long association," Handley wrote in *TV Guide* (1977), "one of the few unforgivable things Dinah ever did to me was being right about 'Shrimp Boats.' It proved to be a far better number for the show than 'I'll Be Seeing You.'"

Jack Gould of the *New York Times* said of the entry: "Relaxed, informal, and running only fifteen minutes at a time, the presentation is a TV tidbit imbued with charm and simplicity."

During the program's first year alone, Handley was faced with the seemingly impossible task of devising backgrounds for almost four hundred songs. He would send Dinah on imaginary excursions to Paris, London, South America, Holland, Mexico or anywhere else a tune might dictate. He borrowed set ideas from cartoons, history, literature, and the movies, and even utilized incidents in Miss Shore's own life to give a song's presentation a new twist. One number, for example, revolved around Dinah's college crush on the school lifeguard. The unfortunate actor playing her beau awaited his entrance underwater in an on-stage pool, and when his big moment arrived, he emerged with blue-hued skin – the liquid had been tinted with dye to simulate depth.

"When you tell a star that on the next show she is to slide down a fireman's pole and her reply is, 'Can I wear slacks or do I have to do it in a dress?' then you know you're working with a *real* star," said the director to *TV Guide*.

"Not long ago we developed a show in which Dinah was to play three famous women of history: - Empress Josephine, Lucretia Borgia, and Pocahontas. "I told Dinah that, somehow, each costume and hair-dressing change would have to be made in twenty seconds. It would mean frantic dashing around and a good deal of nervous tension, but it had to be done.

"Dinah threw an 'Okay' over her shoulder and that was the last I ever heard of it. There were no complaints and no self-pity. Dinah did the job."

Another program involved the use of dry ice to create a big cloud while the singer crooned "Outside of Heaven." From his control booth, Handley thought the effect looked enchanting. Dinah walked through the cloud, singing, and it made a perfect picture. Then the director became aware that his star was singing with more conviction than usual. A mistiness was in her eyes that he hadn't noticed in rehearsal when the dry ice was absent.

It wasn't until after the show that he found out that dry ice, while creating a beautiful effect, removes much of the oxygen from the air. Handley: "The band and the first three rows of audience were practically unconscious. Dinah, who was right in the middle of it, nearly suffocated. But she finished the song and the show."

Afterward, when Hanley told her what had happened, the star's only comment was: "The scene looked fine, though, didn't it, Alan?"

Each show, Hanley tried to do something that was unexpected – from utilizing upside-down sets and double images of Dinah to having The Notables, the show's singing quintet, get up on the studio ceiling to form a mobile.

His only gripe about Miss Shore: "When I need her for rehearsal, she's in her dressing room surrounded by friends, who might include anyone from the president of her record company to a song plugger. And while I'm frantic about the precious minutes rolling by, Dinah refuses to be ungracious enough to walk out on them."

She, thankfully, never failed to make a show, but on the other hand, Hanley never failed to worry either. Though Dinah was always reliable, her voice wasn't. In November of 1953, just two hours before a telecast, the songstress was suddenly silenced by an attack of laryngitis. Rather than cancel the show, which featured Johnny Desmond as its guest star, Dinah decided to be innovative and let the viewers in on what was going on. Ergo, the details of her problem were quickly printed on cue cards, which she held up in front of the camera, while she mouthed the words sung by her chorus. Reading like a roadside advertisement for Burma-Shave, the cards said:

"Hi!"

"I can't talk."

"Lost my voice somewhere."

"Will *definitely* find it by Tuesday."

After the program, she was flooded with congratulatory calls, to which she scribbled on a pad: "I'm at a loss for words."

"Mwah!" – that farewell kiss of Dinah's that became her trademark – came about almost accidentally on one of her earlier shows. Getting into the sign-off theme one night, she heard the producer tell her, "We're late. Throw them a kiss or anything," which she did. On the following program, she failed to repeat the kiss-off and, as a result, was swamped with protests. Thus, her special "goodbye" became a regular part of her repertoire. Only once in her years with Chevrolet did she leave the kiss out, and that was in 1959 when a chimpanzee had her laughing so hard, she could barely catch her breath.

Settings on the NBC variety show would often reflect both Hanley and Dinah's interest in art. Many backgrounds were patterned after the styles of Picasso, Gainsborough, Grant Wood, Raoul Dufy, Eugene Berman, or Georgia O'Keefe. One high school art teacher wrote: "After seeing your show, our students had an astonishingly greater interest in art." Conversely, another viewer offered: "If that stuff is modern art, then I'm a monkey's uncle."

"I'm strictly a Sunday painter," was Dinah's assessment of her own artistic endeavors. "Too stiff to be any good, but it sure is a lot of fun."

She'd taken up the hobby in 1950 after seeing some works of actor Van Johnson, but her first "masterpiece" was so covered with protruding paint that Robert Cummings commented, "She didn't paint it. She chewed it."

Some lessons and one hundred twenty-five canvases later ("They're stashed away in closets all over the house and out in the garage and in George's hair."), she was still not too enthusiastic about her work, yet quite proud of the fact that she'd actually sold two efforts.

In 1953, Dinah was the subject of an episode of Ralph Edwards' "This Is Your Life." Lured to the program under the pretext of introducing her mentor, Eddie Cantor, she was surprised by the emcee who, during the thirty minutes, reacquainted her with many friends from her past.

Among the guests who traveled from Tennessee to be with her were Louise Hammett, her co-star on the old WSM show, "Sweet and Hot," and cousin Dodie Bittner Jaffe: "I brought along a photo of Dinah in the old roadster she used to drive. When she saw it, she said, 'Thank God it's a Chevrolet!'"

"I have no special formula for success," Dinah told the press about this time, "but I feel that all people who succeed have a few fundamentals in common. Desire or ambition isn't enough – you have to have something to sell, and this has to be able to stand up against the competition in your field. But getting to the top and staying on top are two different things."

When asked what she felt contributed most to longevity in show business, she replied, "Two things come to mind. The first is an ability to accept criticism. You can't listen to just the things you want to hear. You must be able to examine what you are doing objectively in order to develop. I've been fortunate in having people around me who have told me what I most needed to hear.

"I think good manners play an important part in success. I mean by that – consideration of others. It may sound corny, but I don't think you can do better than follow the golden rule. You are bound to have clashes with people – differences of opinion. But if you always listen to the other person's side and try to understand his point of view, you'll be easy to work with and well liked."

**

In 1954, the Montgomerys moved from the San Fernando Valley to Beverly Hills so they would be only fifteen minutes away from NBC's Hollywood studios. While George was supervising construction of their new Canon Drive home – complete with fourteen rooms, seven baths, and a seventy-foot swimming pool – the couple sold their Encino house and rented one from movie mogul Jack L. Warner.

Dinah maintained a full-work schedule, but was determined to give daughter Missy a normal home life. The change in residence made it possible for her to be at the house by five-thirty every evening for dinner.

The little girl was just learning to talk when, at bedtime one evening, Dinah began singing her a lullaby. Suddenly, Missy began to cry, pressed her small hand against her mother's mouth, and said: "Tell me a story, Mommy. Don't sing." Baffled by her daughter's reaction, Dinah discussed the incident with sister Bessie, who offered, "Don't you see? Missy associates your singing with going to the studio and leaving her."

Missy caught Dinah off guard again one day when she came home from school and announced, "I know who you are. You're Dinah Shore."

At a loss for words for a few seconds, the songstress finally answered, "Why, of course I am, darling. Didn't you know?"

Missy didn't reply, but looked very angry.

"But mostly I'm your Mommy," said Dinah.

"You sing…Whenever you're Dinah Shore, you sing. I don't like it!"

Dinah picked the five-year-old up, hugged her tight, and the next day took her down to the studio so she could watch how the show was done. As they were walking toward the artist's entrance, several fans started coming toward Dinah, begging for her autograph. "Leave her alone," shouted Missy. "She's not Dinah Shore today. She's my mommy!"

It was outbursts such as these that made Miss Shore vow to be an attentive mother. She and George would be up in the morning for breakfast with Missy, then the singer would drive her daughter to school. Unless one of them were out of town or at an engagement, neither parent ever missed the evening meal with the youngster, and they regularly put her through reading, writing and spelling drills to make sure she was grounded in the fundamentals.

"Children must have a feeling that their mother will be there when she's needed," explained Dinah. "You simply can't compartmentalize your time, because you'll never know when you'll be needed."

Dinah and George arrived late at a party given by the Jack Bennys one evening because, as the singer explained to the hosts, "Missy was acting naughty and I had to punish her."

Guest George Burns, overhearing this, quipped: "Dinah's idea of punishing Missy is singing her a song *not* in the top ten."

By 1954, Dinah was doing only two radio shows per week – both sponsored by Chevrolet – but weekdays remained packed with activity. Mondays, she rehearsed her video show of the following day. Rehearsal continued on Tuesday, right up until the 4:30 show time. After the program signed off, she, along with Ticker Freeman and other production personnel, conducted a postmortem and also went over plans for the Thursday show.

Wednesday was an easy day – only a radio show, followed by art lessons and a couple sets of tennis. Another television program – with its hectic schedule – followed on Thursday, and then there was the week's final radio broadcast on Friday. "I'm torn all the time being so many different people," Dinah admitted at the time.

Both George and Dinah made a pact when Missy was quite young that aside from George's movie work, which occasionally took him off on extended location jaunts, neither of them would be out of town for more than four days at a time. Commenting on this decision, Dinah explained: "You can't take chances with the security of your home. The affection of the television audience is very gratifying. It would be terribly hard to give it up after all the years I've put in building my career. Thank God I haven't had to make a choice as yet. But if the time for choosing ever comes, I won't hesitate for a moment to take the side of my home."

Dinah's fans considered her to be the closest thing to an angel; her co-workers found her a delight to be with; and George, according to the press, was devoted to her – although he did admit to a few pet peeves: If only she would learn to pick up her clothes, be more careful in writing down his phone messages, and less sentimental about birthdays and holidays, his wife would have been perfect. "And when she cooks," he added in jest, "it looks as if a cyclone had hit the kitchen. Takes four pans to scramble a few simple eggs."

Jack Smith, who now appeared solo with her on the radio show, could once have had a reason for a small gripe with Dinah also. Dinah was an inveterate gum chewer, and would always have a stick or two in her mouth at rehearsal. She often went on the air without disposing of it. During one duet, she stuck the wad behind Smith's ear. The gag may have been a bit disconcerting for Jack, but afterwards everybody had a good laugh.

The Montgomerys never intended for Missy to be an only child, but for some reason that doctors were unable to discover, Dinah didn't become pregnant again. Knowing that Missy yearned for a sibling, Dinah raised the possibility of an adoption, telling George: "She's a happy little girl, but she's alone, and that's not good for any youngster."

George was hesitant. The thought of adopting a baby was foreign to him, since he came from a large family of fifteen. He claimed that in Montana, people didn't adopt children. They used the "do-it-yourself" method. Nevertheless, after mulling the idea over until he was comfortable with it, George agreed. The couple put in an application. It was two years later when the Montgomerys finally received a phone call from the doctor who told them that he had located a baby.

Born March 3, 1954, John David Montgomery – nicknamed "Jody" – joined the household in May. He was a bright child who, unlike Missy, didn't seem to mind as he grew older that his mother was a major celebrity. Jody, in fact, rather enjoyed the extra attention this relationship brought him. Like many children, he went into the lemonade business at an early age. When asked by tourists if he was Dinah Shore's son, he'd reply, "Buy some lemonade and I'll tell you." Mother may not have approved of his methods, but she certainly had to admit that she had an enterprising lad.

Though she wasn't an advocate of spanking, Dinah made an exception once in Jody's case, when he was about six. They were at a party when the boy pushed another child into the swimming pool. After fishing the frightened youngster out, Dinah gave her boy a thorough tanning on his backside. Jody was startled by his mother's violent act; he threw his arms around her and began to cry. "Perhaps I should have spanked my children more often," the singer said later. "Somehow there are times when I simply can't control them."

**

With his thriving furniture business and two or three films per year to keep him occupied, George was anything but idle while Dinah was working. True, the movies he appeared in were nothing to get excited about, but they did furnish him with a generous income apart from what Dinah earned, and made him a star in his own right.

He'd left Fox in the late forties and was now headlining one "B" action picture after another – most of them were westerns for Columbia. For the record, some of these epics were *The Sword of Monte Cristo* and *The Texas*

Rangers (1951); *Cripple Creek* (1952); *The Pathfinder; Jack McCall, Desperado;* and *Fort Ti* (1953).

His notices were seldom raves. Two reviews in the *New York Times* give insight to what many think is the reason why he was never able to successfully make the transition to bigger-budget pictures. Commenting on *The Texas Rangers*, the paper said: "He hams it in standard western fashion"; and, regarding *Gun Belt*, a 1953 feature he did with Tab Hunter at United Artists, the remark was: "Mr. Montgomery, by now a thoroughly prairie-broken practitioner of justice, probably is the most authentic and unintriguing buckaroo on the screen today."

At home, though, George was very much the super star. Dinah said of him, "George has perspective. He's able to stand off and see things as a whole, and now I manage to do it too, thanks to him. He's the ballast in our family. Of course, we disagree. Life would be pretty dull without differences. We argue and discuss, but we don't fight. We try to keep emotion out of the argument and find the middle course."

Awards and titles continued to be bestowed upon Dinah. She was named the "Most Glamorous Mother of 1952" by the Los Angeles Downtown Businessmen's Association; Nashville proclaimed "Dinah Shore Day"; and she also received a few more "best dressed" awards.

Being the entertainment industry's "best dressed" lady was flattering, but it also caused her problems, which Dinah commented upon, tongue-in-cheek: "When I went to get the award, I almost couldn't go, because I didn't have anything to wear," she said. "The honor changed my whole life. Now, every time I think of going outdoors and lying in a hammock, I stop and wonder if this is what Miss Tasty Dish of All Time would be wearing to lie in a hammock. I mean, what's the use of lying in a hammock if you're not togged out in your Lying-in-a-Hammock ensemble? What would the neighbors say, not to mention *Harper's Bazaar?*...

"Also, I used to do the marketing in slacks. Now I'm scared to do the marketing at all. Someone'll be sure to snitch to the proper authorities if one pleat is just a little less than reet. I'm a haunted woman, that's what."

Of a more serious nature was an encounter Dinah had with the Internal Revenue Service over her wardrobe. The Montgomerys objected when the tax agent refused to let her deduct the cost of the expensive ($300-$700 each) gowns she wore professionally. The IRS man, on the other hand, argued that although they could only be used once on television, the songstress might then wear them on social occasions.

"Impossible!" said Dinah. "These gowns are skin tight and I can't sit down in them."

"Prove it!" said the dubious government representative, throwing down the gauntlet.

She invited the agent out to the house that evening and modeled one gown after another for him. "Darnedest fashion show I ever saw," recalled George. "Here was Dinah, stooping, squatting and panting as she tried different chairs, and giving the tax man a big sales talk at the same time. And he was studiously observing her through his spectacles, taking notes – he was perfectly serious about the whole thing."

By the time the agent departed, Dinah had earned a sizable tax deduction and the IRS had what has come to be known as "the Dinah Shore ruling" (i.e. a dress can be deducted from income tax returns as a business expense if it's too tight to sit down in).

***

Though Dinah's association with the Columbia label had produced a number of hit recordings, it only lasted four years. Her trusted advisor, Manie Sacks left Columbia in 1950 to return to RCA Victor and, since she'd really signed with the company to work with him, she decided to make the switch also.

"I was Dinah's replacement at Columbia," says Rosemary Clooney. "One of her last acts at the company was to refuse to record a new song with Sinatra – 'Peach Tree Street.' She was absolutely right. It was a terrible tune, but Frank was angry that she'd refused and asked, 'Who was the last girl singer Columbia signed?'

"That was me. I got to do the record."

Back at RCA, Dinah recorded a number of tunes that made the charts – "My Heart Cries for You," "A Penny a Kiss" (with Tony Martin), "Sweet Violets," "Whatever Lola Wants," "Love and Marriage," "Chantez-Chantez," and "Fascination," her last disc to date that made the *Billboard* record chart.

(One interesting assignment she garnered at RCA was to fill-in for Ethel Merman on the Original Broadway Cast album of Irving Berlin's *Call Me*

Madam. Miss Merman, who'd starred in the 1950 smash-hit musical, was prevented from recreating her stage success on records, owing to an exclusive contract with another company.)

When, in 1955, she discussed the reasons for her declining record sales, Dinah took an optimistic view: "This won't last forever. I think the public wants to discover some new people, and the more unusual the style, the better. But, once they discover them, they still want to discover some still newer ones.

"We just haven't been picking our songs correctly, I guess. But one thing I'm sure of – you can't sing down to people. All you can do is sing the best you know how and refuse to compromise on quality. You may hit a smaller audience, but sooner or later they'll come back to you."

Dinah would remain with RCA until almost the end of the decade, when their relationship seemed to deteriorate.

"I was the West Coast representative of the music publisher that controlled 'Scene of the Crime,' one of Dinah's last turn-table hits," reported Harvey Geller of *Billboard*. "To promote the RCA recording, I got her to perform it on her show and, afterward, hosted a party for disc jockeys at the NBC studios in Burbank.

"When Dinah was late arriving, I went down to her dressing room. She informed me she didn't want to attend the party. She was tired and there were just too many people to meet. I *insisted* she go, since this was, after all, a 'Scene of the Crime' party, but I promised I wouldn't leave her side. She was too shy to go up by herself.

"The next day, I ran into an RCA exec who'd been at the affair. He said that after a few drinks he'd gotten up enough nerve to tell Dinah she was no longer with RCA. They were dropping her. Her records weren't selling, and they felt she was uncooperative. She avoided doing promotions with disc jockeys. Even getting her to perform her own records on the air was a chore.

"I saw Dinah a few days later. She told me that *she'd* decided to leave RCA, and wanted to know if I could recommend another label. I told her I'd think about it."

This, unfortunately, was the era of rock, and from now on, the lady who'd never become as solidly identified with a single waxing as did some of her competitors was going to find her recording career in a fairly steady decline.

She'd certainly had a good run though, with a total of nineteen million-record sales since the early forties.

***

The television medium was different. In this field Dinah had a constantly growing audience and, though harder work than films, radio or records, she found its informality tailored for her and stimulating: "I have a hard time remembering words, especially if I *try* to remember them. If I made a mistake only I know about, I let it go. But if it's something obvious, you can make a gag out of it. That's what I like about television. You can make capital of your own mistakes."

Bob Banner joined Dinah's video family in 1954, replacing Alan Handley as producer-director of her twice-weekly show. A tall Texan, Banner had previously been associated with such television fare as "Omnibus," "The Fred Waring Show" and "Garroway at Large."

"I first met Dinah while she was renting a house from Jack Warner," says Banner, "and I remember thinking that this lady would have become important in any profession she went into. She was practical, literate, persuasive, and she knew what she did well.

"Dinah was also analytical of what others contributed. You couldn't ignore her enthusiasm…her exuberance. She was truly interested in people, a good listener, and trusted those colleagues she respected."

Soon after Banner came aboard, The Skylarks also signed on – replacing The Notables. Begun in Detroit back in the mid-forties by George Becker and Gilda Maiken, this quintet had sung with Woody Herman, Harry James and Jimmy Dorsey before Banner spotted them on the bill with Dean Martin and Jerry Lewis in Atlantic City. Personnel in the group had changed somewhat over the years. The roster for Dinah's show, aside from George and Gilda, included Earl Brown, who would later be assigned to write special material for the program; Joe Hamilton, the future producer-husband of Carol Burnett; and Jackie Joslin, a native of Nashville. As one of the singers described her first impression of Dinah: "She really couldn't be *that* nice. She had to be a phony. But she wasn't."

It was a relaxed atmosphere working on the fifteen-minute show, and practical jokes between performers and the production staff were the order

111

of the day. Banner: "Dinah tried to learn the lyrics to all her songs because she felt that when they were written on cue cards, she lacked spontaneity. However, many times on the air she became unsure of the lyric and really needed the cards, so it was a good thing we'd made them up – even though she'd said not to do it.

"Finally, Ticker and I decided we'd teach her a lesson. The number was 'Mountain High, Valley Low,' and this time we had the cards written in Arabic.

"When she saw them *on the air*, Dinah broke up, grabbed the cards from the crew member, and showed them to the audience. It was a most charming moment on camera.

"With Dinah, I was never worried about things going wrong. Usually her flustered state worked well for us."

The singer always seemed to turn the potential disaster in favor of the program. One show had a production number in which Dinah was to be pulled in a boat across a stage covered with dry ice. Regrettably, the ice melted before air time, but rather than let the misfortune throw her, she made a gag out of it. "You see, folks," she said before she went into the song, "we were going to do this in boats, but a funny thing happened…"

Leo, the MGM lion, was an occasional guest on Dinah's show, and more than once, was used by a mischievous staff member to play a gag on someone. Gentle as a kitten, the beast was, nevertheless, frightening enough in his looks to scare even those people who knew he was tame. "At the end of one program," chuckles Banner, "we had the lion's trainer instruct Leo to jump into Dinah's lap. She knew that he was harmless, but was still afraid to push him off. She did her whole final number that night sitting down."

Then, there was the time that three chickens got loose on the stage while Dinah and guest Andy Williams were singing "Canadian Sunset," prompting several disbelieving viewers to write in and ask, "Did we see chickens pecking about on the show the other night?"

Dinah answered the queries on the air: "I'm sorry, but you must be mistaken. NBC doesn't allow animals in the studio." Yet, just as she said that, two black cats crossed the stage behind her.

More mail arrived, resulting in another reply: "I don't understand these letters. As I said before, there is a network rule. *No* animals are allowed in the studio." Just then, Leo the lion crossed behind her…and the cycle continued.

Earl Brown of The Skylarks: "I'll never forget the show when Dinah and I were waltzing and singing 'Three O'Clock in the Morning.' The heel of my shoe kicked a platform and – one right after the other – all the pillars on the set toppled over."

It was the studio versus the control booth on many of the pranks that were pulled. Dinah and orchestra leader Harry Zimmerman got together on one that had Banner and the entire control booth staff panicked before air time.

Sitting in the sound-proof, glass-enclosed booth, the director couldn't understand why he was not hearing either Dinah's singing or the musicians' playing. The microphone switches were on, and the star was there on the stage in front of him crooning her number. Yet, no sound was coming through whatsoever.

Of course, there was no real problem. Once Banner went into the studio, he saw that Dinah wasn't really singing – just mouthing the words – and Zimmerman and his men were only pretending to play.

"We got our revenge," says Banner, "on April Fools' Day, when we set all the studio clocks ahead five minutes. The three minutes of mayhem created by cameramen and performers rushing to get into place was hilarious."

Under Banner's direction, Dinah broadened her talents and tackled things she'd never tried before. One unusual program employed the services of Peter Foy, the man who'd made Marty Martin fly in *Peter Pan*. Bob informed his star that she would be sailing around on wires above the studio's hard cement floor, and her only reply was, "Good!"

"When I first started on the show," Banner reports, "Dinah was apprehensive about dancing, but I got a couple of top choreographers – Tony Charmalee and Nick Castle – to work with her and she quickly became good, even in complicated routines."

In May of 1955, Dinah introduced a new song on her show entitled, "I Was Too Busy," with words by the late Frances Case Hopkins of Columbia, Tennessee, and music composed by Joe Hamilton of The Skylarks. This was a poignant piece – a mother lamenting that she'd never taken the time to enjoy her children as children. It received a favorable response from the viewers and, as a result, the songstress repeated it every Mother's Day.

Ask any of her friends to describe Dinah Shore, and one of the first words they'd use is "generous." She was truly a giving person, not only of material things but, more importantly, of herself.

Rosemary Clooney recalled the time that she and her then-husband, actor Jose Ferrer, accompanied George and Dinah to a nightclub in Hollywood to see the late Billie Holiday: "Billie was spaced-out – paranoid by then – and interpreted Dinah's openness as being phony. Her tragic life had made her wary of people who were that open. Dinah recognized this and, rather than take offense at Billie's negative remarks, was kind enough to just let them pass."

Miss Clooney debuted her own NBC show in 1958 and, awaiting her when she arrived to do the initial program, was a hand painted scarf from Dinah. "I have a very warm, affectionate feeling toward her," said Rosemary.

Miss Shore's sensitivity could even extend to a person she'd never met. Watching a novice girl singer go off-key on a television program, Dinah could see that the girl was obviously distraught and she rushed to the phone to call the station. "Please give her a message," she told the stage director who answered. "Tell her that what just happened to her could happen to any singer and does happen to most one time or another. It happened to me once and I thought I was going to die. Tell her she has a beautiful voice and that her career should be just beginning. Tell her this is very unimportant and wish her luck."

The 1956-57 season was a decisive one for Dinah. Possessing an endurance record unmatched by any other lady singer on television, she was pressured by her network to drop one of her two weekly quarter hours in favor of doing an hour special every month. It was NBC's method of testing the extent of her popularity – to see if she might have the potential to carry a weekly hour variety program, like Perry Como was doing then.

"I was dragged into it screaming," she admitted. "I liked my fifteen-minute show. I was happy with it and I don't like changes."

Broadcast from New York, the special entertainments received fine notices from the nation's critics and gave Dinah the opportunity to work with such important guest stars as Dean Martin, Marge and Gower Champion, Perry Como, Art Carney, Count Basie, and Stubby Kaye. Charles Mercer, writing for the *Associated Press*, said of the one hour entry: "Miss Shore carried the whole thing effortlessly...It will be a great misfortune indeed if someone at network, agency or sponsor level fails to set into motion the process of bringing us Miss Shore more often in hour-length shows next season."

Not surprisingly, that's exactly what Chevrolet wound up doing.

8.

The Chevy Years

"TV was invented for Dinah Shore," is the way one columnist summed up the songstress' impact on the public from 1957 to 1961. He wasn't alone in his assessment. With her immensely successful variety show, it is said that she virtually "ruled the Sunday air."

She'd done a total of 444 of her fifteen-minute programs when she dropped that format altogether in the autumn of 1957 to begin work on her live full-hour color entry for NBC. Chevrolet was picking up the tab for twenty-four segments, which would run through the season opposite such popular video fare as "General Electric Theater" and "Alfred Hitchcock Presents." The budget for each show was $145,000.

"I'm not intimidated," she said of her competition. "TV's a live, responsive medium with personal contact and pressure. I respond to it. I guess it's the hambone in me."

Not long after her debut, the entertainment industry knew that fifty million viewers preferred to stay tuned to NBC at nine on Sunday evening; the attractive and vivacious performer had captured the major audience, thus becoming the first member of her sex to headline a hit weekly variety show.

Attempting to explain her success in this male-oriented genre to *TV Guide* (1960), Dinah said: "Right from the beginning, they wanted me to be a female emcee. And right from the beginning that's one thing I've fought against. It's a man's world, and thank heaven for it. Neither men nor women like to see a woman out there in front running things. On those occasions when I absolutely have to introduce a guest, I sort of slide into it. I just don't want to be that awful word, a 'femcee.'"

The caliber of guest on "The Dinah Shore Show" was an important factor in insuring the program's longevity. Stars like Frank Sinatra, Hugh "Wyatt Earp" O'Brian, Gwen Verdon, Yves Montand, Roy Rogers, Shirley MacLaine, Betty Hutton, Boris Karloff and other seldom-seen faces on the tube, added to the songstress' ratings when they appeared with her.

How was Dinah able to attract such elusive talent when other variety programs could not?

It wasn't only the ten thousand dollar fee they were paid, since most of the top shows offered that. "When an act or an entertainer comes on our show," disclosed the singer, "our choreographers and arrangers sit down and create special material just for them – tailored specifically to the guest's style, not mine.

"For instance, if Ethel Merman and I do a song together, it's a song in Ethel's idiom – not mine. This does many things. First, it makes our show a perfect showcase for guest stars, which allows us to compete successfully to get talent. It also gives the show one more dimension.

"The creation of a special number for me to do with a guest is the big difference from 'getting into the act,' which is an intrusion on your guest's talent and usually comes off as a baggy-pants lampoon of his art. That's why we are so very careful, so very respectful of our guests."

Unlike many weekly variety hosts, Dinah was perfectly content to do the very best with her own solos, then serve as a willing, cooperative and helpful foil for her guests. When Sinatra made his first television appearance with Miss Shore, her staff choreographer devised five dance routines from which "ol' blue eyes" was to choose only one to perform with the hostess.

118

Nevertheless, so that her guest's selection would be easier, Dinah learned them all, went through each with Frank, then accepted his decision as to which would ultimately be used.

"That Sinatra show was a classic," said Bob Banner. "He and Dinah performed a medley of songs they'd done in the past. The chemistry was perfect."

Former ball player Dizzy Dean was another who received special treatment. Complaining that the script contained so much dialogue that he was uncomfortable, he received a sympathetic hearing from producer Banner, who ordered a major rewrite.

Her admiration for talent even led to Dinah's tackling a fifteen-minute dramatic scene from *Affairs of Anatole*, with Academy Award-winning actor Joseph Schildkraut: "I didn't want to do it at first. He was just too good and I felt that I was sort of intruding, holding him back. But he worked with me with the patience of Job. He almost literally pulled me up to somewhere decently near his level. He had me doing things dramatically I never thought I could possibly do."

Charles Laughton guested on one of Dinah's Christmas shows. Portraying campaigners in India of the old school, complete with pith helmets, the couple performed a rousing tune in the English music hall tradition, "We Want to Be in England for Christmas."

"Relaxed" was a common adjective employed by writers to characterize "The Dinah Shore Show." How else could one describe a program on which singer Guy Mitchell felt free enough to kick off a shoe; stoic Boris Karloff let go to warble "Mama, Look at Boo-Boo"; or Nanette Fabray, playing a musical saw in a feathered dress of Dinah's, decided to saw-off a protruding plume that got in her way.

Dinah: "The show flows easily because we prepare it for a month and rehearse it thoroughly. We go over our lines and songs again and again until they are so much a part of us that we don't have to ask, 'what comes next?' By the time we're doing the program, we can have fun because we *are* relaxed."

To help instill this warm feeling with her guests and regular co-workers, Dinah, always the accomplished hostess and gourmet cook, would occasionally prepare lunch for the entire crew in her studio dressing room. Ray Bolger was so taken by this practice that he told about it on the air, and Peter Lawford even sent her a new refrigerator. "I have to do something to keep up my modesticity," she said.

Practical jokes were kept to a minimum on the expensive Sunday-night show, but what was absent in planned laughs was made up for by a series of amusing impromptu happenings over the years – many of which had to do with Dinah's accidentally discarding some of her clothes on the air.

Rob Banner shudders when he remembers the night that, in order to accomplish a quick change, Dinah wore one dress over another – the top one being held together by magnets: "She got out of this prop car and the entire front part of the garment pulled off. Thank God she had the other dress on underneath, or we'd really have been in trouble."

Another staff member recalls a similar situation: "She was singing 'Cry Me a River,' wearing a low-cut dress and leaning forward toward the camera. What she didn't realize was that *everything* was showing. "Ticker was frantic – writing a message to her on cue cards – but Dinah remained totally unaware of what she was exposing."

Perhaps the best-publicized incident of this sort occurred on October 9, 1960, when Red Skelton was the show's principal guest. Dinah had just completed a twenty-second costume change for a sketch with the comedian when the dress zipper, which ran the length of her back, popped open. "Turn around and show them the zipper," Red suggested with a grin.

Grasping the dress together, she spun around quickly, as Skelton ad-libbed, "This might be the biggest show of the day."

"It'll be in the flesh," shot back the hostess.

"Call your friends!" shouted Red to the howling audience.

A safety pin was used to make a hasty repair, after which Dinah immediately went into the next act – a folk dance. Unfortunately, when her dancing partner spun her around, the dress opened again, exposing her bare back to the audience for a brief moment. She quickly moved off-camera, where fifteen straight pins closed the breech, then she returned to complete the number.

"We've had lots of goofs over the years," an assistant said later, "but never anything like this."

Because of the time difference, Dinah's program was done live for the East Coast, then aired via kinescope recording for the West three hours later. As a regular practice, the show's key personnel would gather at the

Montgomery's Beverly Hills home each Sunday at about eight to view and critique the program. They'd have a few drinks, a bite to eat, and generally unwind after a hard week of work. Sometimes the tired guests might get a little carried away after the nine o'clock broadcast and, in fact, every few weeks one of them would utilize the pool for a midnight swim in the nude.

"George wasn't always happy we were there," reported one guest. "Why should he be? He wasn't really involved in the show. Usually about ten o'clock he'd make it clear it was time for us to leave. He'd give us a mild hint like turning the lights on-and-off, or taking all the coats out of the bedroom and tossing them onto the living room floor. He wasn't angry. He was just kidding, but on the level."

Dinah's reaction to her husband's calling curfew: "She just smiled and looked embarrassed."

She, evidently, became a bit more upset with George during a business trip to Hawaii. "We were out to dinner at a nice restaurant," swears the witness. "I believe there were the Montgomerys, and four or five members of the show staff. When the check came, Dinah was kicking George under the table to pay it. He didn't."

Like the situation with her parents, the Montgomerys differed in their attitudes toward money. Dinah found it almost impossible to live within her budget, while George behaved as if the banks were going broke. He controlled the family finances with a tight rein, supervising all expenses – from food to his wife's clothing. One rumor that circulated claimed that he refused the housekeeper's request to buy a washing machine, saying "If my mother could do the laundry by hand, so can you."

"I remember visiting Dinah and George once when they had the house on Canon Drive," said a business associate. "The place was beautifully decorated. You could tell that Dinah had a hand in it. Only one thing was wrong. The couch and other living room furniture had plastic covers over them. I could understand that George wanted to cut down on the furniture cleaning bill, but it made the place look 'tacky.'"

If George and Dinah were having marital difficulties at this time, one wouldn't have known by the numerous news stories that were being fed to the public, extolling them as "Hollywood's happiest couple."

"What most people take for granted is what I have to work the hardest for," Dinah would tell interviewers. "My family means more to me than anything in the world – nothing will ever interfere with that. The rest is velvet. I have only one fear – that if the time comes when the public no longer demands me and being a wife becomes a full-time job, I'll not make as much of a success of it as I have of the part-time one. Right now, I'm a successful career woman. In ten years, I'll tell you if I'm a successful woman."

A tennis enthusiast who played nearly every weekend, Dinah finally gave it up in favor of being with her kids: "It was a Sunday morning and we were down in Palm Springs. I had a game of tennis in mind, but it didn't seem to materialize. Instead, George and I spent the day hiking, riding and painting with the children. I think we both suddenly realized, without anything actually being said, that the tennis was shutting us off from Missy and Jody. I haven't played very much since, and really haven't missed it. You move on to new interests, and it's infinitely more rewarding to share those interests with your children. They grow up pretty fast, you know, and the first thing you know, they're gone."

Tragedy struck the Montgomerys in the mid-fifties when, following a trip to the Hawaiian islands, Dinah lost what would have been their second *natural* child. Seven months later, she was back in the hospital again briefly for what was described as "minor surgery."

***

Though George's career as the star of "B" action movies was thriving, he seemed to remain in his wife's shadow. She always expressed a keen interest in his work – both in films and in his furniture business – and, whenever possible, tried to shift the publicity spotlight over to him. But, realistically, how could quickie theatrical efforts like *Masterson of Kansas* (1955) or *Last of the Badmen* (1957) hope to get the same kind of newspaper space as one of the most popular variety programs in the history of television? George had the almost impossible task of trying to shake the title, "*Mr.* Dinah Shore."

Perhaps the best opportunity he had to raise his acting fortunes was by way of his own television series, "Cimarron City," an hour western which aired over NBC during the 1958-59 season. Sadly, the show had a difficult one-year run since, during the second half-hour, its competition was CBS's perennial "Gunsmoke."

Even Dinah tried vainly to make her husband's series a success, appearing briefly with their two children in a segment patterned after Dickens' *A Christmas Carol*. Nothing seemed to help though, and when the NBC schedule for 1959-60 was announced, "Cimarron City" was absent from the listing.

There were other outside TV guestings for Dinah besides the Western. On November 27, 1955, for example, she assumed the hostess duties for an episode of "The Loretta Young Show," and twice in 1958 she played herself on segments of Danny Thomas' CBS comedy series. Daughter Melissa, in fact, joined her in the second of these shows. Of more importance, however, was her 1957 appearance with such stars as Pat Boone on the "General Motors 50th Anniversary Show."

Dinah, with all her television work, still tried to keep busy in nightclubs whenever time would permit. June of 1956 marked her Las Vegas debut at the Riviera Hotel. Also on the bill were The Skylarks who, along with the star, commuted by air to Los Angeles during the engagement in order to do their video show.

Variety said of the act: "...it's the perfection with which Miss Shore embraces the superbly designed repertoire that rockets her act to that star plateau of entertainment."

So tremendous was the audience and critical response to the Vegas date that, less than a year later, she was back at the Nevada resort, commuting daily, this time from the Flamingo Hotel. It was a rigorous schedule she was putting herself through – flying back to California at three each morning – but she thrived on the nightly offerings of "Blues in the Night" and "It's So Nice to Have a Man Around the House." She said: "Sometimes I feel so tired during a routine like this I want to go home to my little family and stay there forever. But it's sorta funny. You can really lose yourself in front of people who want you. I sing and I'm not tired anymore – or maybe it's the singing that makes the being tired worthwhile. When I feel the house is with me, I get goose pimples."

Fifty thousand dollars was paid to Dinah for her Flamingo gig, but almost more important than the money was the bonus the engagement offered her – an opportunity to try out possible numbers for her NBC program. It might be said that this was one of the most lucrative (to Dinah) public rehearsals on record.

If awards and honors were any criterion, then the "world" loved Dinah Shore in the years she was on Sunday nights. Testimonials and citations were continually heaped upon her until they all seemed to melt together into one huge mass of adoration. In 1957, she and Perry Como were named America's "King and Queen of Hearts" in a poll of the nation's disc jockeys, conducted by the American Heart Association. The lady was also saluted as the City of Hope's "Mother of the Year." B'nai Brith cited George and Dinah in 1958 as "Mr. and Mrs. American Citizen," then, that same year, she was announced by the Hollywood Women's Press Club as the most cooperative actress. (Tony Curtis received the masculine counterpart.) About twelve months later, she garnered the Genii Statue from the Radio and Television Women of Southern California. And the show-business fraternal order known as The Masquers "roasted" Dinah in April of 1958. Emceed by Pat O'Brien, the tribute was paid by such celebrated personages as George Burns, Allan Jones, California Governor Goodwin Knight, and Ethel Merman. The latter said of Dinah, "She's the nicest, kindest, most considerate performer I ever worked with. Long may the queen of television reign."

She also became the first woman saluted by another private show-business club – the New York based Friars – in a roast that carried the theme, "Dinah, you're a square!" And when then-Vice President Richard Nixon commented on the late Senator Estes Kefauver's campaign for the Democratic presidential nomination, he'd said: "If we have to have a candidate for President of the United States from the state of Tennessee, I would nominate Miss Dinah Shore."

When, in 1955, the Academy of Television Arts and Sciences presented its first Emmy to a female *singer*, Dinah won it, and she achieved the honor again in 1956. She also took the first award presented to a female *personality* (1957); "Best Continuing Female Performance in a Series by a Comedienne, Singer, Host, Dancer, Emcee, Announcer, Narrator, Panelist, or any Person who essentially Plays Herself" (1958); and two more similar statuettes a year later.

The Gallup Poll found her to be one of the Ten Most Admired Women in the World (along with Jacqueline Kennedy, Eleanor Roosevelt, Mamie Eisenhower, and Queen Elizabeth); and she won honors from *Radio-TV Daily* and the Hollywood Foreign Press Association, as well as the Sylvania and Peabody Awards.

It wasn't all accolades for the singer, however. In 1958, she was admonished by Democratic Representative Frank Chelf of Kentucky to sing "My Old Kentucky Home" the way Stephen Foster wrote it – or not at all. Crusading for a year against efforts to reword Foster's lyrics to avoid such expressions as "darkies," the Congressman became upset when Dinah sang his state song on her NBC show in a revised, non-dialect version. "She's had plenty of time to reply to my letter of protest," said Chelf, "but hasn't even had the courtesy to do that.

"It could have been her sponsor's idea to change the words. That's General Motors. I've been driving a General Motors' product for years. Maybe I won't buy anymore."

The remarks didn't seem to affect Dinah, who continued to sing, "See the USA in your Chevrolet…" to a steadily-increasing audience each week for a reputed salary of twenty thousand dollars per show. ("I don't get quite that much and, anyway, I don't get it in straight salary.")

Continually interested in attempting something new, the songstress tried her hand at straight dramatic acting in March of 1961, devoting one of her Sunday programs to an adaptation of Noel Coward's *Brief Encounter*. Written for television by Joseph Schrank, the video version changed the original British modern setting to Boston of 1908 – mainly so Dinah would not have to perfect an English accent. Her co-star in this bittersweet tale of a love affair that never really gets started was Ralph Bellamy, who, in his pre-Broadway days had played the Orpheum Theater in Nashville.

"I don't know if I would do it without Ralph," said Dinah. "He's our Rock of Gibraltar. You know, after all the musicals, I've found that the hardest thing about doing this play is that I have to think."

Writing in the *Los Angeles Times*, Cecil Smith said of the program: "Although technically the production had a gloss and a sheen rare for television, the tender story of an unrequited middle-year romance seemed curiously unmoving. Perhaps the fault lay not in the play but in its stars. Neither Dinah Shore, making her dramatic debut on television, nor Ralph Bellamy seemed to give their roles more than competence – there was no tug at the heart."

Another try at something different had taken place a couple of seasons earlier when "The Dinah Shore-Chevy Show" had featured a number of unknown acts from other countries. "The foreign attractions gave us a new look," Dinah claimed. "And any show that's been on the air as long as we have needs one. A show gets a whole new outlook when it imports acts from other nations. Many of the European and Asian stars we've brought over have never been on TV before and they have a different approach to the medium than Americans."

One of the hours, for example, was tagged "South Pacific Holiday," and featured native dancers and singers from Bali, Moorea, Samoa, Tahiti, Fiji, New Zealand, and Australia. Comic Jonathan Winters was also on that show.

Miss Shore and her producers must have been doing *something* right. She continued to hold her gigantic audience through all the various innovations and even numbered then-President Eisenhower as one of her loyal fans. The First Lady had told Dinah, "When we're at home, Sunday night is always Dinah Shore night at the White House."

With all the new devices employed on the program, the consensus in the industry was that it was still the star's deft handling of her guests which made the real difference. "We want to make sure the guests enjoy each other, that they're happy and at ease," she'd continually expound as the seasons went by. "The show is like a party. I like people to have a good time at my parties.

"Of course, it helps to have the audience comfortable and relaxed. I remember a time one of the McGuire Sisters became ill just before the show. I had to improvise, even sing her part. And I had to keep the audience from becoming alarmed.

"I managed all right, I guess. I refuse to be panicked. I just thought, 'if I goof – or somebody else goofs – well, that's all right; I'm not going to die.'"

Week after week, Dinah and her staff, which by 1959 included Bob Finkel as producer and Dean Whitmore as director (Bob Banner had left the show to pursue his own projects), got together to kick around fresh ideas on how to best utilize upcoming guests. "Take Art Carney," she explained to *TV Guide*, "he must never be presented as just himself, because there are so many different kinds of things he can do. He's got to be Ed Norton and Art Carney and half-a-dozen others. Why we even had him sing 'Everybody Loves a Lover' and do a soft-shoe dance. He was adorable.

"Louis Jourdan, who opened the 1958-59 season for us, has a natural fear of being just a handsome straight man for other people's jokes. We were careful to give him lines and situations that made him into something besides the typical, hand-kissing continental. And for Maurice Evans, we had to find a light but dignified way to lead him into one of his readings. We take care of these things."

Singer Mahalia Jackson, extremely moved by the red carpet treatment accorded her on "The Chevy Show," said to the hostess, "You are the realest person I know."

Jimmy Durante, Betty Grable, Marge and Gower Champion, Danny Thomas, Bette Davis, Esther Williams, Shirley Temple, Sid Caesar, Ginger Rogers, and Ella Fitzgerald were only a few of the many other celebrities charmed by Dinah's special treatment, yet she found that the guest she had the most trouble booking was husband George Montgomery. He did appear from time-to-time, but these were usually programs that featured other couples – such as Steve Lawrence and Edie Gorme – as guests.

"Over the years, she was marvelous about working with stars who were not particularly her favorite," recalled Bob Banner. "Our main criteria in choosing people to be on the show was 'who was important at the time,' and 'who would complement her well.'"

"My big problem in being the female star of an hour-long show," said Dinah, "is finding the right male stars I can bounce my lines off without being the aggressor. Our guest stars must have, above all things, authority...The better they come off, the better I come off."

Aside from her natural warmth and relaxed qualities, there was another well-known aspect of the Shore image – a more material aspect.

Over half the fan mail the singer received concerned her television wardrobe, a collection of fifty-five breath-taking gowns and dresses each season. Most of her clothes were designed by Bob Carlton of NBC, but, on occasion, Dinah would take a European holiday, both to enjoy the time off with her family and to buy a new wardrobe for her next season. During the run of her program, she wore originals designed by such leading dressmakers as Balenciaga, Givenchy, Balmain, Chanel, and the Fontana sisters. Annual costume budget for the show (including Dinah, cast, and guests, who often wore their own clothing) was $85,000.

Carlton: "A single costume can, and often does, take three or four days to construct. Though it is usual for a custom design to call for four fittings, we usually have to do it with two, sometimes one."

All of Dinah's outfits met one major requirement – they were equipped with back zippers to facilitate a fast complete change of outer clothing between numbers. Exact length of time she had to perform these "miracles": between twenty and sixty seconds.

"Every time I go through one of these quick changes, I'm terrified," she admitted. "When I step back on stage, and see that camera on me, I pray I'm fully clothed. Sometimes I'm caught pulling or tugging, and there I am – no place to hide. I tell everybody what's going on, smooth my skirt, and go into a number."

Dinah decided to fool her audience on one program and thereby prove that one didn't have to wear an expensive dress in order to look nice. Hence, the November 20, 1960 show featured the star in a number of attractive outfits – none costing more than $29.95. ("As long as I feel good and look good, it doesn't matter what a dress costs. I often buy something inexpensive to make up for spending so much on a few."

Summing up her image as the well-dressed television star, Dinah said: "If people do find me glamorous, maybe it's because I accept myself. It would be nice to think you mature emotionally with the years. I know I'm not afraid to be myself now. And I think if you have that self-acceptance, people don't notice if a hair is out of place.

"Femininity is an attitude. It's a feeling you give out. It's not merely your bust measurement."

Despite statements like these, one of her closest friends told *Time* that "deep down she's insecure. Everything that's happened to her is so good that she's afraid it will disappear tomorrow. So she drives hard all the time."

The star did confess to possessing a temper, though not a violent one: "I'm not a shouter, though I may be a sulker. I sulk when people say I'm a great personality but not much of a singer. I'm a good singer and I work hard at it – and my feelings get hurt." Whatever Dinah's minor personality faults might have been, they didn't stop her from being a valuable asset to both NBC and Chevrolet. People in the entertainment industry, in fact, credited the success of her Sunday show in enabling the network to build its huge facility in Burbank.

Claimed Bill Powers, advertising manager for sponsor General Motors: "Dinah is our *number one* salesman. I'm convinced she could sell anything to anyone."

Dinah also seemed happy with Chevrolet: "Our sponsor is very proud of the show and hence doesn't live or die by the ratings. You just do the best you can."

It, therefore, came as a shock when, in February of 1961, Dinah announced that she and her sponsor of ten years had parted company. A spokesman for Miss Shore said: "The deal they offered was different from those of past years. They wanted her to be hostess for a series of big specials to tie in with sales drives and promotional campaigns.

"Dinah felt that she is a performer first and a saleswoman second. She didn't want to be an adjunct to the General Motors sales department."

Money definitely was not the issue. The manufacturer had been more than willing to pay Dinah the same fee she'd earned for doing a season of shows in exchange for her headlining only eight or nine heavily sales-oriented specials per year. As far as the major portion of the rest of their television advertising budget was concerned, it would be invested in a new NBC Western series, which would, hopefully, reach a segment of the television audience that didn't watch Dinah. The name of that new series was "Bonanza."

Dinah had no problem finding someone else to sponsor her series. She was in a position to pick and choose, thus making the transition a smooth one. (Ultimately, advertising spots were divided between American Dairies and S&H Green Stamps.)

Other troubled areas of Dinah's life, however, were not to be placated so easily, and within the next year or so her mythical kingdom of happiness would crumble.

9.

The Bubble Bursts

THE ANNOUNCEMENT WAS MADE IN EARLY DECEMBER, 1961, JUST A FEW days short of their eighteenth wedding anniversary. It stunned the public. It stunned the people with whom they worked. It even stunned their closest friends. "Dinah Shore and George Montgomery have separated," is the way their spokesman put it. "Attorneys for both are arranging the divorce. Mr. Montgomery is no longer living at home. There is no dramatic reason for the split and the decision was reached without rancor by either party."

What went wrong with Hollywood's "ideal couple?"

"Marriage was so sacred to Dinah," said a good friend, "she could have made such a decision only after a lot of soul-searching. It would have taken something earth-shattering to make her take such a drastic step."

Despite conjecture from those who knew the pair, Dinah and George had made a pact to divorce with dignity. For their own sakes and the benefit of their children, there would be no public casting of aspersions. A settlement of their approximated two million dollars in community property would be handled as peacefully as possible through attorneys and an amicable arrangement reached regarding custody of the children and accompanying liberal visitation rights. As expected, Melissa and Jody would remain with their mother.

The first real insight into the causes of the split came in May of 1962, when the songstress appeared in Santa Monica Superior Court for the divorce hearing. Charging "mental cruelty," she told the judge that she became very lonely because her husband spent much time away from home. She singled out instances of absence during Christmas holidays of 1959-61 when George was in the Orient for several weeks. "I asked him not to go on the last few occasions," Dinah testified, "but he refused."

Continuing, she complained that when she and her husband entertained guests, he would "spend long periods of time on the phone and be very rude to our guests. He would also absent himself and go back to his own room and not appear again."

Dinah claimed that she'd offered to accompany George on his trips, but he'd replied it would be a "great inconvenience for him – and just wouldn't work out."

Summing up, Dinah said: "I lost weight…and it became difficult for me to perform my duties both as a mother and as a performer."

The lady had testified to the manifestations of her unhappy situation, but what had caused these problems to develop in the first place?

That Dinah's career accomplishments had far surpassed those of George was certainly a contributing factor. It didn't matter that he had built a successful furniture manufacturing company, had worked steadily as a well-paid actor, or that through his keen business sense and the advice of experts invested both his and his wife's earnings to the point where they'd become millionaires. The outside world cared little about this. All they knew was that Dinah was one of the biggest stars in show business and George was a performer in second-rate westerns.

It must have been a painful situation for George, though he handled it remarkably well, never trading on Dinah's success to achieve his own goals. Perhaps the beginning of the end of the marriage was written when Montgomery, in an effort to "spread his wings" and establish a new image for himself in the movie industry, decided to co-author, produce, and direct his own picture, which would be shot in the Philippines. He'd discovered how inexpensive it was to make a film in that island nation back in 1956, when he'd worked there for United Artists in an actioner called *Huk*.

The Steel Claw (1961) was released by Warner Brothers and had George, who was the only American name in the cast, playing a Marine Corps officer fighting with Philippine guerrillas against the Japanese. Reviews were not good. Said *Variety*: "Montgomery undertakes the taxing four-ply assignment of producer-director-writer-star, but is not particularly successful in any of those departments…As director, he exhibits a taste for hard-fighting, hard-drinking, hard-loving behavior, but his perception of personal relationships is awkward and two-dimensional."

"George has a serious fault in that he tries to do too much by himself," a friend told *Good Housekeeping* back in 1962. "Two years ago, Dinah gently tried to persuade him that he should not try to write, produce, direct and act in his first motion picture effort. She pointed out that money was no problem. They could well afford experts for at least two of the chief responsibilities.

"Stubbornly, George insisted in having his way. When the picture was previewed, Dinah did her utmost to focus attention on George's achievement, even though the picture was mediocre at best.

"It was a bad evening. When the film was over, everyone clustered around Dinah. The sight of George, standing apart, almost alone, while Dinah tried to maneuver her way to him through a mob of chattering sycophants illustrates to me how they were constantly being thrust apart by pressures neither of them could control."

According to Dinah: "The real problem with my marriage was that we were too bright with each other all the time. We couldn't tell each other our troubles. The whole world had an image of us and so did we, a beautiful Technicolor image. We never quarreled; he never knew what deeply troubled me and I never knew what deeply troubled him. If you don't share your private distress and sadness, there is something fundamentally wrong with the relationship. In the end, we just drifted apart."

This lack of an in-depth dialogue between the partners was certainly the doing, to a large extent, of Dinah, whose memories of her parents' angry verbal battles during her childhood made her determined not to repeat that history in her own marriage.

Taken individually, the differences in personality between Dinah and George (he was a saver, while she liked to spend; he was a day person, but she enjoyed nights; and so forth) would not seem to be sufficient cause for *major* disharmony in the marriage. Yet, lumped together with all the other incompatibilities – and without open lines of communication to relieve the tension – it was only a matter of time before something had to give way.

There had been rumors for some time that Montgomery was not only trying to date some of the chorus girls working on Dinah's television show, but he was also keeping regular company with women other than his wife. One of these ladies was the lovely blonde actress Diane McBain, who said, "I sincerely doubt that the few dates I had with Mr. Montgomery did anything to break-up his marriage. In fact, he was already separated at the time."

A few people in the know reported that Dinah was romantically involved for a while with a man who would become a prominent television producer and the husband of a popular star. Indeed, according to Earl Brown, who had become a confidant of Dinah's, her aforementioned "minor surgery" in the mid-fifties was actually a termination of a pregnancy, the result of that affair.

Whether the tales of George's extra-curricular activities were true or not, some friends of the couple seem to feel that what finally broke the marriage was an attractive brunette actress from Israel named Ziva Rodann.

Miss Rodann, who denied being responsible for the split, had been hired by Montgomery to co-star with him and Gilbert Roland in another Philippines-based movie for Warners, *Samar* (1962), which concerned the Filipinos' struggle for independence against Imperial Spain. Again, George handled the same four creative chores he'd tackled on *The Steel Claw*.

"In the fall of 1960," Miss Rodann told an interviewer, "I joined the company in Manila. There were only five Americans in the cast. We all stayed at the same hotel and naturally became close friends. I sensed that George was a deeply troubled man. During the three months of filming, his communications with Mrs. Montgomery seemed to be almost entirely about the business aspects of the picture. On the other hand, George spoke frequently in loving terms about his children, who he sometimes called by long-distance telephone."

While he was in the Orient, George made a business trip to Hong Kong and there, according to the press, had a luncheon with Ziva, who'd flown over from Manila during the short lull in filming – ostensibly to play tourist.

Halfway through their meal at the exquisite restaurant, they were interrupted by a loud voice coming from the foyer that bellowed, "There she is!"

The diners in the room looked up to see an obviously angry man rushing to the table where the film people sat. "So this is what has been going on!" the man bellowed.

He was Prince Raimondo Orsini, the wealthy Italian playboy, who at one time had squired Ziva around Rome. Smitten with the beautiful actress, he'd flown to Hong Kong to visit with her, then became incensed when he found her in the company of another man.

The tirade continued in Italian and broken-English, with the Prince finally looking at George and declaring, "I challenge you to a duel! Pistols will be the weapon. You will hear from me later."

Both George and Ziva were dumbfounded as they watched the Prince stride proudly out of the dining room. A duel in 1960? Who ever heard of such a thing? The matter was quickly resolved without bloodshed. Ziva explained to the hot-tempered Orsini that George was merely her employer and that this had been a business meeting. The Prince apologized, but the incident was not easily forgotten.

"Once the story made the papers, everybody got going on the marriage," said a family friend. "Dinah took it as long as she could. When George came home, they had it out."

What actually happened between the Montgomerys when George returned from the Orient was only for them to know. Neither believed in airing their "dirty linen" publicly, thus the matter was buried for several months, until the shocking December 1961 divorce announcement.

"We are only good friends," said Ziva Rodann when asked of her relationship with George. "Anything more is foolish talk."

Following the divorce, Montgomery continued to appear in films of the same meager caliber as those he'd made throughout his career – including several more that were shot in the Philippines. He also took a fling at the legitimate theatre, starring around the country in such plays as *Two for the Seesaw, Under the Yum Yum Tree* and *Plain and Fancy*. Additionally, he was seen in a series of national television commercials for a leading furniture polish, which prompted Hollywood comics to quip: "George Montgomery and Euell Gibbons [the late naturalist] are forming a vaudeville act. Montgomery will make furniture and Gibbons will eat it."

George never remarried, however in 1963 he was involved in a situation that caused him some embarrassing newspaper headlines. On August 27th, a distraught lady threatened him with a pistol in his Van Nuys home. The weapon fired when he tried to take it away from her. Nobody was injured, but the assailant, a former maid of the Montgomerys, was tried and convicted of misdemeanor assault. She was placed on probation. Interestingly, at her trial the woman testified that she'd been "intimate" with George on several occasions in 1961 and had committed her desperate act only because he'd spurned her love.

***

The end of her eighteen-year marriage wasn't the only major problem Dinah was forced to contend with in 1962. Ticker Freeman, the songstress' arranger-accompanist for the past twenty-three years, left her employ in June, stating that his demand for a "substantial raise" had not been met by Henry Jaffe, who was then serving as producer-packager of Miss Shore's NBC-TV shows.

Since Dinah was now appearing in only nine hour-shows per season, instead of the more than twenty she'd done before, Ticker's income had been cut accordingly and, as a result, he'd accepted some outside assignments, including work arranging Eleanor Powell's nightclub act.

The reasons for his departure were quite practical and understandable, yet that didn't change the fact that Dinah was sorry to see her longtime friend depart. Without his help and encouragement during those rugged early days before she hit on radio, she might never have achieved her then present lofty position.

In the wake of her personal troubles, Dinah continued to work, concentrating heavily on her television shows and an occasional nightclub engagement. These personal appearances were especially difficult for the singer during the initial months after the separation because she was never sure which songs to sing. One of her aides recalled: "About the only song she could do at that point that wouldn't have a double meaning was 'The Star-Spangled Banner.' Dinah identifies completely with anything she sings and some of her standards suddenly became pretty tough – songs like 'It's So Nice to Have a Man Around the House,' 'Hello, Young Lovers,' and all those others. She was well aware of this but decided to just go ahead and do them. If the audience wanted to read anything into them, that was their privilege."

The singer began playing tennis more often – usually every day – and also took up golf. Additionally, she found time with her reduced television schedule to reevaluate her career, her life-style, and her relationship with her children. "Every performer has a public image," she once said. "Mine unfortunately, was one of perfection. It's an impossible thing to live up to. We all of us have our human frailties, only I wasn't supposed to. If anything good can be said to come from a divorce, it has at least made more of a human being out of me in the public eye."

As a result of her soul-searching, Dinah made an important decision. In January of 1963, she announced that she was taking a "leave-of-absence" from television – effective the 1963-64 season – and would not consider appearing regularly on the tube for a least a year. "I've been on a regular schedule since I was six years old," she said, "and I want to devote more time to my family." Melissa was then fifteen and Jody was eight.

The children, as might be expected, had taken the divorce rather hard. Missy had gone into tears when told, and her mother comforted with, "Have a good cry. I had one, too."

"I'm not crying for me, Mommy," sobbed the youngster. "I'm crying for you."

Dinah was speechless.

She finished her nine shows for the current season, which featured such guests as Bing Crosby, Bobby Darin, Ella Fitzgerald and Andre Previn, then threw a farewell party for her co-workers. Staff-member Earl Brown remembered the depressing affair: "We were doing that program from New York and nobody really knew if she was really going to quit or not. Near the end of the evening, she made the announcement – 'Well, that's it. It's been lovely,' – or something like that. She didn't have to say anything else. We all knew what she meant. It was a real 'down' evening. I felt like I'd lost my own family that night."

Determined to get herself and her children away from their Beverly Hills goldfish bowl lifestyle, Dinah sold the family home and moved the clan to Palm Springs, where she could devote her entire time to being a parent. "I used to sing a song called, 'I'm Too Busy,'" she would explain. "It tells of a mother who asks where her children are. Suddenly she realizes it was twenty years ago since they played around the house – that they're gone! She'd been too busy even to learn to play with them. One day I looked around and found myself in the same situation as the woman I'd been singing about. Missy was fourteen and in high school – a beautiful, wonderful young lady. I wanted to get to know her and spend time with her before it was too late. And Jody was growing up, too; he was getting so tall and big, and was going into the second grade.

"A career in television is very demanding. While at the studio I used to say, 'I want to be sure I'm home when Missy and Jody get there.' When I got home, I'd feel I had left everything undone at the studio. I was always thinking I should be somewhere else. I never seemed to be around in an emergency – and whenever children need you it's an emergency. Missy would come home from school with some emotional problem, and I wasn't there to listen and give her advice when she needed it most. By the time she saw me at six o'clock, she'd talked it over with someone else.

"Nowadays, the demands on my time are Missy's and Jody's. It isn't just going to be PTA meetings, and getting up and having breakfast together. It's that vital moment when you have to be there, or you don't get another crack at it. If I miss those precious moments, I won't have been a real mother."

***

Dinah's divorce became final on May 9, 1963. Seventeen days later she surprised almost everyone by marrying again. The groom was forty-two-year-old Maurice F. Smith, a well-to-do building contractor who'd wooed and won the lady on the Palm Springs tennis courts. He also had two children by a former marriage.

Joined together by a judge in Redlands, Miss Shore wore a sleeveless white crepe dress with matching bolero. Missy was her mother's maid-of-honor and Smith's eldest son, Dexter, was best man. The newlyweds spent their honeymoon driving through Northern California, then set up housekeeping in the Palm Springs area.

It was a union that was not to last, however. Approximately one year after their wedding, the new Mrs. Smith filed suit for divorce in Indio, California, alleging "mental cruelty." She said in later testimony that Maurice had "consistently criticized" everything she said and did, and her family and children as well. His comments were such that she "couldn't make an independent decision."

(Friends of the couple claimed that Maurice was furious when Dinah decided to accept some club and television dates, rather than stay at home.)

Though there was talk of a reconciliation, Dinah was, nevertheless, awarded her interlocutory decree in August, 1965. A month later, Smith filed a countersuit, claiming that the lady had committed adultery with several men during their marriage.

"The charge is outrageous," she commented through a spokesman. "It is utterly and completely false – and the matter is in the hands of my attorney."

Said her lawyer, Deane Johnson: "What puzzles me is what Smith and his attorney really want. If they are sincere in that they really want a divorce, all they have to do is petition the court for the final decree."

Smith never made his motives public, but in October asked the court to dismiss his suit, thus clearing the path for Dinah's receiving her final decree.

Still a true romantic in her mid-forties, Dinah had quite possibly married Smith in a desperate attempt to achieve her dream of an ideal marriage. ("I just know it's there, I really do. I've seen one or two or three really happy marriages, where people give to each other, respect each other, live in terms of each other. Seeing even a few makes you realize, God, it must be possible. What a wonderful way of living and thinking and feeling – to be able to give and take selflessly.")

She refused to say anything whatsoever about her union with Maurice Smith, and her friends referred to it simply as a "disaster."

***

Missy gave Dinah cause for concern in September of 1963. The fifteen-year-old was riding with three friends early one Saturday morning when their automobile smashed into two parked vehicles in the Palm Springs area. Miss Montgomery, who was not driving, received severe cuts and bruises on her face and body, as well as a broken nose. Dinah stayed at her daughter's bedside, and George drove down from Los Angeles. A later suit against the car's driver garnered Melissa a $10,000 settlement.

Dinah was a proud mother in 1969 when Melissa Ann became the bride of actor-producer David Lee Burke. Sadly, this marriage didn't work, but the girl later wed again. The second groom was Mark Hime, son of a Beverly Hills jeweler and, in April of 1974, the couple became the parents of a daughter, Jennifer Trinity. "I think she is the most beautiful child in the world," said grandmother Dinah, "but, of course, I'm prejudiced."

Career-wise, Dinah Shore maintained a low profile during most of the sixties – compared with her activities of the previous two decades – but she was anything but idle. Lucrative nightclub engagements and other personal appearances kept her busy several weeks a year, yet also allowed plenty of free time to relax and to be with her family. There were well received engagements in Las Vegas (at such plush hotels as the Riviera and the Sahara), Lake Tahoe and an extremely successful 1967 booking at the Waldorf-Astoria in New York. She was also seen a couple of times in the Greater Los Angeles area – with Bob Newhart at Anaheim's Melodyland in 1963 and with The New Christy Minstrels at the Carousel Theater in West Covina during 1966. Of the latter engagement, Clyde Leech of the *Herald Examiner* said: "Miss Shore did everything she has ever done in the field of entertainment except sell an automobile and did it all superbly well."

Audiences who attended her Carousel show saw a somewhat new Dinah. Not only did the songstress treat them to a medley of her standard ballads and blues numbers, but she also went a bit modern with a few up-tempo tunes strongly influenced by Bossa Nova and The Beatles. "Jazz is no longer a singer's medium," she noted. "It doesn't have the beat that a singer needs to hang on to. And there was a period when I was really worried about the way pop music was going. When rock 'n roll first started, it was very primitive. 'Careless Love' and 'Itty-Bitty Bikini' were the most involved lyrics they knew, and we all wondered just what kind of music our kids would have to look back on when they grew up.

"Then came The Beatles. I was a fan of theirs from the first…even when they seemed a kind of a put-on. They got the beat back and they had humor, often a very finely satirical sardonic kind of humor. Their chord changes and their progressions and all those things are excellent. The kind of music they've produced is the most exciting we've had in the last five years."

Dinah also tried her hand at singing with a full-fledged symphony orchestra again, departing in June of 1968 with her own conductor, drummer, and bass player for a multi-city tour to work with these high-brow groups. It had been almost twenty years since she first sang with a large orchestra, which had featured two or three times the number of musicians that usually backed her on television or in clubs, but the memory of that initial experience was still unsettling to her. "I was singing 'Blues in the Night,'" she remembered, "and suddenly there's this thump – a great big old womp – and it's all those strings coming in, right on tempo. That big old blast of strings liked to blow me right off the stage. I looked back with a start and the audience broke up."

She went to Rio de Janeiro that same year – along with Paul Anka, Elmer Bernstein, Sammy Cahn, Nelson Riddle, and others – to represent the United States at the Brazilian Music Festival. She also became the National Easter Seals chairman, visiting then-President Johnson in the White House to kick off the annual campaign.

Though Dinah would almost consistently draw capacity crowds wherever she appeared during the sixties, she found that no matter what she seemed to try by way of recordings, her discs just weren't huge sellers. After leaving RCA late in the 1950's, she'd signed with Capital, where she recorded a number of unsuccessful albums with the likes of Andre Previn, Nelson Riddle, and Red Norvo conducting the orchestras.

Reprise hired her next to cut a blues album, appropriately tagged "Lower Basin Street Revisited." By having the songstress croon such pieces as "Basin Street Blues," "More" and "Nashville Blues," the record's producer had hoped to attract the nostalgia buyer who would want to hear Dinah sing the type of tunes that had made her famous. The album was not, as they say in the trade, a "mover."

There was a 1967 LP for Total Sound Records ("Songs for Sometime Losers"), then Dinah signed with Decca in 1968 to try something a little different – an album of country-western songs, waxed in Nashville. Producer of that album was Owen Bradley, her former pianist at WSM. Titled "Country Feelin'" the pleasant entry featured the singer interpreting compositions by such artists as Bobby Goldsboro, Jan Cruchfield, and Buck Owen. It, too, did little to enhance her reputation as a money-making recording artist.

Television was an altogether different situation. In this medium she retained her charismatic drawing power – both as an occasional guest on other artists' variety shows ("Guesting on someone else's show is not for me. It never comes out quite like it was presented to me. The ultimate choice is not really mine, except maybe for the songs I'd sing."), and as the star of several specials. After hostessing three daytime and four evening dramatic-theme (geriatrics, child molesting, etc.) programs for Purex beginning in late 1964, the lady went on to headline some unique one-shot, night-time musical entertainments that were well received by audiences and critics alike.

One of these, airing in early 1965 over ABC-TV, featured Dinah and Harry Belafonte in a previously taped, multi-lingual concert for Peace Corps volunteers who were awaiting their overseas departures. "We had a time learning some of the languages," commented the singer, "and I'm still not sure what some of the words mean. The Swahili really swings, but I needed more time for my Iranian."

Another program originated from the Los Angeles Music Center and featured Bob Hope, Laurindo Almeida, Henry Mancini, and the UCLA Chorus and Glee Club as guests. In a comic duet with the hostess, Hope tagged her as "the Mary Poppins of Song."

Dinah didn't appear to be in top form for this telecast. *Variety* reported: "The special lilt and melody in the voice of Dinah Shore seemed strangely absent from two of her singles..."

Two years later, on a "Kraft Music Hall" special seen over NBC-TV on Thanksgiving Eve 1967, Miss Shore paid tribute to her hometown in an hour entertainment dubbed *The Nashville Sound*. Guesting on this multi-musical flavored show were Eddy Arnold, the Everly Brothers, Johnny Mercer, Ray Charles and the Stony Mountain Cloggers. "Don't ask me to explain the theme," said Dinah. "It's just there, like the sun and the moon. And the funny thing is, the 'sound' always has been there, only people in the music business are just now discovering it.

"People seem to think that Nashville music is all country and western. It isn't, any more than it is the blues, or ballads, or anything else of one kind. They're all rolled up into what I call a feeling, a different tone and timbre."

As pleasing as the Kraft program was, it was not as interesting an entry as the two-part special Dinah had starred in earlier that year for CBS, which focused on the Moscow State Circus and was shot in Minsk, Russia, over a two-week period.

She arrived in the Soviet Union – with five new fur coats – to learn that she'd planned her wardrobe wisely. The temperature was eight below zero.

Her duties on the show were to work with a variety of circus acts – jugglers; bears; Popov, the world-famous clown; spirited Cossack horses; and high wire performers – but the incident that really raised everyone's eyebrows is when she accepted an invitation to step into a cage to feed a brace of untamed Siberian tigers. ("The circus manager screamed bloody murder and the producer had his cast insurance cancelled.")

Dinah will never forget the night prior to her departing Russia when she and her American colleagues were the honored guests at an intimate little affair at which vodka was a prime refreshment: "They began drinking toasts to us, and I was determined to uphold the drinking honor of America. Unfortunately, I am not a drinker, nor were my associates. The Russians toasted, 'to peace; to friendship; to the artists of the world,' and I'm trying to drink vodka for vodka with them. After a few vodkas, I started making up the toasts. 'To this great loving spirit between us,' I say, I made up toasts they never heard of. That's what they tell me I did."

Discussing the changes that had affected television since the days of her weekly program, Dinah offered: "It was a different time when we were doing the Sunday show. Emotionally, it was a Gary Cooper time, a period of reticence, of holding back. You couldn't express full depth in a song, either a sad song or a funny song. This kind of openness would embarrass an audience. In a nightclub, yes – there you could go all out. But not in front of the cameras.

"Today, on TV or anywhere, you can say something emotionally when you sing simply because the audience wants you to feel. Today, they let you wear your emotions in public.

"Maybe I've matured. Maybe I'm just not afraid of emotions anymore."

With her television appearances cut to just three or four shots per year, Dinah began to see the truth in the adage, "Fame is fleeting." A New York cab driver, for example, thought he recognized her when she climbed into his vehicle, saying, "I know you! Aren't you Doris Day?"

Even more disturbing was when she arrived at NBC Burbank's facility ("I built that studio. The first orchestra ever used in those buildings was for my show.") to tape a cameo spot on "Laugh-In." Stopped at the gate, the guard looked at her without recognition and asked, "Name, please?" Dinah stared the man straight in the eye and replied, "Leslie Uggams."

"Yes, Miss Uggams," he said. "Go right in."

"She did one of the funniest bits we ever had on 'Laugh-In,'" recalled the show's star, Dick Martin. "The entire stage was decorated in beautiful drapes and scrims: Billy Barnes was at the piano; and the announcer said, 'Ladies and gentlemen, Miss Dinah Shore.' She walked in – dressed in an exquisite gown and looking like she was going to sing – then just passed by the piano and went off. It was priceless."

Dinah had moved the household back to Beverly Hills in the mid-sixties, and one of her frequent escorts during that period was Dick Martin, who'd known the singer since 1956. She'd first seen him on the bill with his partner, Dan Rowan, at a Los Angeles nightclub. Later, she signed the team to star in her July-August replacement series, "The Chevy Summer Show."

"I dated Dinah between her *serious* boyfriends," said the comedian. "Everytime we started to get romantic, I'd get booked into Reno and when I got back she'd be involved with somebody else. Finally, I sent her a wire: 'If we're going to get serious, I can't play Reno anymore.'"

Actually, Martin could take credit for giving Dinah the basic idea that eventually led to her popular talk-variety show: "I took her to the Emmy Awards the night 'Laugh-In' walked-off with everything, and while we were sitting there, I suggested that since she owned most of her old programs, she should do an afternoon 'Dinah Reflects' type of format, featuring guests and clips from the best shows."

It was a valid suggestion that Miss Shore found intriguing, yet it would be advisor Henry Jaffe who would finally convince her that she should make the transition and change her image from that of a singer to a television "personality."

10.
People Will Talk

As in most areas of the performing arts, television has given the back seat to women. Dinah herself had admitted that the biggest video stars – whether in comedy, drama or music – have always been, with a few notable exceptions, of the masculine gender. For every Dinah Shore, Carol Burnett, or Lucille Ball, there are a half-dozen men of equal stature. Even the advent of Barbara Walters didn't seem to have made much difference in the sexual balance.

Although most of the ladies who had made names for themselves in the broadcasting medium had come from the comedy-variety fields, there have been a few over the years who established themselves simply as television "personalities," stars who don't sing, dance or tell jokes, but who simply exhibit sufficient natural wit and charm to captivate an audience. On the tube, the "personality" seems always to be working, if not as a host of his own program, then as a member of a celebrity panel on a game show.

One of the first and most talked-about gals to achieve "personality" status was Faye Emerson. A former contract player of dubious talent at Warner Brothers, who seemed to specialize in "fallen women" roles (*The Mask of Dimitrios, Between Two Worlds, Hotel Berlin, Nobody Lives Forever*), she was once married to Elliot Roosevelt, son of F.D.R. Faye began to make her initial television appearances on both dramatic and game shows during the late forties, and it wasn't long before the enchanting lady was garnering considerable newspaper coverage over the plunging-neckline gowns she wore on the air. Her "The Faye Emerson Show," comprised of interviews and the like, debuted in 1949 for a three-year run. Later, she served as hostess for several other programs and was a panelist on *I've Got a Secret* for five years.

There were a number of female personalities in the early video years. Betty Furness, for instance, was a former Powers model who had had several radio-television shows of her own, yet immortalized herself by standing next to a refrigerator and saying those unforgettable words, "You can be *sure* if it's a Westinghouse."

One-time actress Wendy Barrie (*Dead End, Five Came Back, The Hound of the Baskervilles*) made the personality scene hostessing a program that debuted in 1948, appropriately entitled "The Wendy Barrie Show." An astute and outspoken interviewer, she refused to be "bullied" by her network – ABC – and often revealed to her audience any complaints she might have against her bosses. As a *New York Times* writer once described her: "Wendy Barrie is probably the only television personality who frequently sits on the floor and talks to the viewers. Sometimes she runs the palm of her hand over the rug, patting it gently, and reveals a sudden thought right out loud, 'Gee, this would be a great show for a rug sponsor.'"

Ilka Chase ("Fashion Magic," "Masquerade Party"), Kathi Norris, Lilli Palmer, Arthur Godfrey's sister Kathy (of the 1954 quiz "On Your Way"), Virginia Graham ("Girl Talk"), Anita "The Face" Colby, who was hostess of "Pepsi-Cola Playhouse" (1954), Carmel Myers, and Robin Chandler of "Vanity Fair" (1951) were a few of the women who took their shots in the personality market. Nevertheless, the most successful and perpetual lady of talk in the history of television had, most certainly, been the glamorous Arlene Francis.

Respected as a dramatic actress on stage (*The Women, The Doughgirls, Dinner at Eight*), screen (*All My Sons, The Thrill of It All*), and television (*Laura, Harvey*), Miss Francis had appeared regularly on more talk and game shows than possibly any other member of her sex. She was best known for her appearance as a panelist on the ever-popular "What's My Line," having been involved with that program since its inception in 1950.

In 1952, Arlene presided over a video version of "Blind Date," her old radio program, and two years later was the hostess of "Soldier Parade." That same year, NBC president Sylvester "Pat" Weaver set her to be "editor-in-chief" of "Home," an innovative afternoon show, which publicity releases described as a "women's service magazine of the air." Co-anchored by Hugh Downs, the program ran for over three years before it was eventually dropped despite loud protests from a loyal audience. Critics of the cancellation theorized that the concept of meaningful daytime programming was perhaps ahead of its time.

Despite the numerous cancellations that plague all performers who remain on television for any length of time, Arlene Francis endured more than two-and-a-half decades, setting a higher standard of poise and charm which all other female personalities have strived to achieve.

***

Henry Jaffe couldn't have picked a better time to pitch Dinah the idea of returning to television via a daily talk show. She'd recently been primed for such a proposal when a stranger had bumped into her in an airport and queried, "Didn't you used to be Dinah Shore?"

Even a generous lady like Dinah was capable of a bruised ego.

Her longtime friend had been quite persuasive. "Look, you're spinning your wheels," Jaffe said. "Aren't you tired of Vegas audiences? Don't you want to say something? You're more interesting now than you were ten years ago. Why not do a daytime television show in which your guests would be invited simply to enjoy themselves, with or without heavy talk."

Dinah wasn't sure at first. She really didn't want to work a five-day week, but Jaffe had promised that a full week's worth of shows could be taped in two days. Missy was no longer at home; Jody was away at an Eastern prep school; and a program of this sort *would* be much easier than playing concerts and clubs. If she had any lingering doubts, they were put aside after she spent a week in Philadelphia co-hosting "The Mike Douglas Show," where she had a ball.

NBC-TV, Dinah's old stomping grounds, snapped up the proposal to have her headline a half-hour show for the ladies at nine each morning. It was called "Dinah's Place," and the studio setting – with its wooden beams and red brick floor – was copied from a room in the star's own Beverly Hills home.

"It's an open-end show," she told reporters about the program, which was reminiscent in format of Arlene Francis' old "Home" entry. "All the things women are interested in: mostly how to stay attractive, young, beautiful, thin; how to diet, take care of their husbands and children; how to sew clothes and cook and apply makeup."

Singing on the show was kept to a minimum, much to the disappointment of both Dinah's fans and the press. The songstress, in fact, did only one number each day. The tune she chose for the debut was her Mother's Day favorite, "I Was Too Busy."

"What we are is a 'Do' show," she said. "Almost everyone who comes on has something they want to do. Ethel Kennedy played the piano, Joanne Woodward did some beautiful needlepoint, Cliff Robertson made a linguini, Burt Lancaster did a perfect Italian spaghetti sauce."

Premiering on August 3, 1970, the entry was greeted with a mixed reaction from reviewers. Most critics found Miss Shore delightful, but noted that she refused to be drawn into a meaningful discussion with controversial guests. When James Kavanaugh, for example, explained his marital creative-separation theory, she passed-up the opportunity to take issue with him by not vocalizing her true feelings – that it would be quite difficult to keep a marriage together when the partners are living apart. Time and again she would be too gracious a hostess to play the devil's advocate and, instead, referred to the staid cue cards that were constantly being flashed at her. ("After the first couple of weeks, I was trying to figure out how to get out of it. I didn't know what I was doing and they threw some real curves at me.")

Another guest – a psychologist – told a case history about a wife who got upset when her husband fondled her in the kitchen. Embarrassed and feeling she should say *something*, Dinah cheerfully offered, "Well, that does sound like fun."

"I'm glad we started in August," admitted executive producer Jaffe, after

the program had been shooting for a couple of weeks. "It gives us a long shakedown. Fortunately, nobody is watching us now."

A bright array of stars visited Dinah for some light chatter – Jerry Lewis, Carol Burnett, Jack Benny, Bob Hope, Danny Thomas, and Burt Bacharach, among others. Almost all the guests during those early weeks were old friends. Bacharach, for instance, played tennis with Dinah regularly.

"He's one of the few people who likes to play singles," she muses. "So before I got started on my daytime TV show, I had to make a trip to Japan and I wanted to take drummer Mark Stevens with me, but Burt wanted him for the West Coast production of *Promises, Promises*.

"I told him, 'I'll give you anything, but not Mark.' I couldn't possibly go to Japan and try and sing with all new musicians. So we decided to play tennis for him. I was so sure I'd win I even called Mark and told him not to worry, he'd surely go to Japan. So what happened? I relaxed too much and lost. Now whenever Mark Stevens sees me, he reminds me I lost him a trip to the Orient."

Dinah once learned a Bacharach tune under the composer's careful direction. "One Less Bell to Answer" was its title, and after much painstaking rehearsal, she was positive she had it down pat.

Sometime later, they were at the same party, and she was requested to sing. She chose Burt's song. He accompanied her on the piano. "When I came to a relief part," she reflects, "I looked at Burt and there he sat shaking his head slowly back and forth. Finally, I thought, I'm really getting through to him. While we had been friends for a long time…he never said much about my singing. But I had turned the tide…I thought."

A few weeks had passed before she ran into Bacharach again. "I'm going to record 'One Less Bell to Answer,'" she proudly announced, "because I've never sung it wrong."

"You've never sung it right," replied the composer.

The songstress was flabbergasted. She reminded him of the party when he played for her and sat shaking his head back and forth in approval.

"That wasn't what I meant at all," Burt corrected. "I was shaking my head and whispering to myself, 'wrong, wrong, wrong.'"

Bacharach wasn't the only star with whom Dinah played tennis. She always seemed to have a celebrity crowd at her home for drinks, a bite to eat

and, of course, a match on her court. Friends tagged her house, "Dinah's Bar and Grill."

One player was then-Vice President Spiro Agnew, who'd been making headlines by accidentally bopping spectators on the noggin with his errant golf balls. So, why should he play tennis any differently?

"I still don't know how it happened," said the singer, trying to recall how she came to get a black eye, courtesy of Mr. Agnew's forehand shot. "I was the Vice President's partner, and I was at the net with my back to him when he served. Yet he hit me right in the eye. I've never seen a man so embarrassed. "I'm a Democrat, but that had nothing to do with it."

Dinah wore her shiner for three days.

Agnew would later appear on Dinah's NBC show and play the piano. "Do you play as well as Harry Truman?" she asked.

"I doubt it," he replied.

"How about Mr. Nixon?"

"Never – never, are you kidding?"

More shows were taped and Dinah became more comfortable with her new format. Frank Sinatra came on early in the series and provided what observers consider one of the most charming segments. Refusing to rehearse, he also convinced the hostess that she should forget the cue cards and "wing it." After all, she *was* a "pro" – one of the best in the business.

Conversely, there was the program when her guest was Bishop Fulton J. Sheen, who stared at her so intently that, "I could only sit there and stare back – which didn't make for much audience excitement."

Eventually, Dinah developed her own unobtrusive method for conducting her interviews, which elicited interesting remarks from guests like Barry Goldwater, who advocated that citizens should only be drafted in a war of self-defense; and Martha Mitchell, wishing her son was in Canada rather than Vietnam.

"We don't have the time or luxury to probe," she answered critics who expressed the desire that she seek more depth in her interviews. "We do a show, not a *talk* show. When people appear with me, they are guests in my home – even if I'm at odds with them. I will never try to beat guests down. I can't stand to embarrass anyone – even my own kids. My first reaction when people say something embarrassing is to help them cover.

"I admire people with strong convictions. I listen to all sides here, and I've learned that people with real convictions aren't that far apart in basic philosophy. It's their way of going about it that is different. That's why I can talk comfortably with people who hold totally divergent views. What I don't question is their sincerity, and that's what moves me – the fact that they truly, honestly believe."

One of Dinah's favorite pastimes was cooking, thus it was only natural that a section of each program be devoted to the culinary art. She prepared a pumpkin soup for Vincent Price; Harvey Korman revealed his recipe for burgundy beef balls; Senator Edmund Muskie hypnotized a lobster; and Sinatra made a spaghetti sauce.

"When Bishop Sheen was the guest," she remembers, "I told him I'd cooked fish for him. He looked stricken. 'I eat only one kind of fish and that's filet of sole,' he said. Fortunately, that's what I cooked – filet of sole, no pun intended."

Laying out the recipes was actually the toughest part of the program: "People keep saying we aren't as good as the 'Galloping Gourmet' or Julia Child shows. But we only have six minutes for the cooking segment of our thirty-minute show, while Graham Kerr and Julia have a full half-hour. People think of us as a cooking show and I don't like to dispel that notion because it's enhanced my myth, but it really *isn't* a cooking show at all. In fact, the cooking is quite simply an obstacle course."

Not one to argue with a successful formula, Miss Shore compiled her first cookbook in 1971 *Someone's in the Kitchen with Dinah*, which was published by Doubleday. The volume contained more than two hundred recipes that she'd collected over the years.

***

"I really don't feel I can be alone," Dinah confided to a girl friend during a break in the taping of one of her shows. "I was meant to be married."

A truly meaningful male-female relationship had eluded the songstress after her second divorce. She was never without dates, having innumerable unattached friends of the opposite gender who enjoyed being with her simply because she was good company. Yet, no true romance developed with any of these men. ("There really wasn't anyone special.") Having failed twice at love, perhaps Dinah was a bit hesitant to rush too quickly into a permanent relationship or, more likely, maybe the right guy just hadn't come along yet.

Her well-publicized involvement with Burt Reynolds began in 1971. Much like her romance with George Montgomery, it, too, had started from afar. Dinah had seen the actor on various other talk shows and was attracted to him at once, even though they hadn't actually met. "When he first came on my show," she said in 1972, "I liked him still more. First of all, and obviously, he was a dreamboat. Second, I was pleased to see he had a genuine sense of fun.

"We knew from that first day. Both of us *knew*. We came off camera and walked back to my dressing room and just talked – something you never have time for. He was a *man* – vulnerable and sensitive, funny, mature, warm and empathetic, and all the disparities you might think could be there did not exist.

"After that we met again and finally we began to go steady. I think what binds us together is that we both have a fear and dislike of quarrels. He's Aquarius, I'm Pisces, which means that we just have to live our lives harmoniously; everything else is intolerable. We laugh together, which relaxes me. If he'd been the type of man who likes powerful confrontations, strong discussions, endless arguments, we couldn't possibly have gotten along."

Burt Reynolds had been a familiar face on the Hollywood scene for over a decade when he first met Dinah Shore. A former college football player with looks that would attract most any woman, he had worked fairly regularly in motion pictures and television, but had at that point only flirted with true stardom. Actually, from the standpoint of "stature," the films he was doing in the sixties were really on par with those that George Montgomery had made during the forties and fifties – "B" programmers.

Florida was Reynolds' birthplace. He was born there in 1936, a mixture of Cherokee and Italian blood. His strict disciplinarian father, from whom he was estranged for many years, was the chief of police in North Palm Beach. "Burt was always a fine boy," recalled his mother, "but he had a temper. He'd take just so much, then he would blow up. Every now and again he'd get too big for his britches and his Daddy would have to straighten him out. But that's all it took, a little straightening out, then he was a good boy again."

Once his promising football career had been cut short by a knee injury sustained in an automobile accident during his college years (1955), Burt tried his hand at his second love; acting. He studied at the Hyde Park Playhouse in New York; hung around the Actor's Studio; and, following a season of summer repertory, appeared with Charlton Heston at the New York City Center in a production of *Mister Roberts*.

Television and movie assignments followed. He co-starred with Darren McGavin in the short-lived "Riverboat" series, then played important roles in such insignificant theatrical films as *Angel Baby* (1960) with George Hamilton; *Armored Command* (1961), starring Howard Keel; *Navajo Joe* (1966); *100 Rifles* (1968), featuring Jim Brown, Raquel Welch, and Dan O'Herlihy; and *Skullduggery* (1969). There were also two other unsuccessful television series: "Hawk" and "Dan August," both cop shows. There was also a short stint on "Gunsmoke."

Reynolds tags the movies he made during the sixties as "the kind they show in prisons and on airplanes, because nobody can leave." Certainly the efforts did nothing to enhance his career, such as it was.

Along the way, he had married once. The bride was perky British actress Judy Carne, who would later become known as the "sock-it-to-me girl" on "Laugh-In." The union, which began in June of 1963 and ended three years later was, the former Mrs. Reynolds recalled, "a wild trip. The hostility got so out-of-hand that one day I bought him a punching bag."

Additionally, Burt's luck began to change about the time he and Dinah became an item for the gossip columnists. He completed his first *important* picture, *Deliverance* (1972), a Warner Brothers release by director John Boorman, which was based on James Dickey's novel about four men whose weekend canoe trip turns into tragedy. But prior to its release, the actor made headlines of an even more sensational nature. He posed nude (with his hand strategically placed) in *Cosmopolitan* and became the favorite pin-up for thousands of women all over the country. ("I did it for fun, also to get some publicity. I also did it for free.")

The stunt proved to be a wise career move for Burt. Overnight he found himself to be a household name. His bargaining position was strengthened by some fine personal reviews for his performance in *Deliverance*, and he became an in-demand actor.

Dinah had been against the idea of her boyfriend posing in the buff: "I'm basically shy and withdrawn," she admits, "and can't stand any open displays of strong emotion. I also don't like exhibitionism. It's totally against my nature. When Burt told me about the nude centerfold, I was mildly shocked. I thought it was a very bad idea. Bad for his image, worse for mine. I said, 'No, no, no, don't do it, it's a crazy idea.' He said, 'It's a first. I think it'll work. It's going to be *funny.*'

"Well, he went ahead and did it anyway. You can say I was overridden. I waited for the proofs, feeling pretty damn awful. The day he brought them home I was afraid to look at them. Then when I finally saw them I had to laugh. I just fell over! I realized the whole thing wasn't at all distasteful. It was simply the biggest put-on of all time."

When the photo first broke, the couple were in Chicago where Burt was appearing in a legit production of *The Rainmaker.* Dinah's response to the obvious questions from the press: "It doesn't do him justice. He has a much prettier smile."

The May-December affair, which must have fascinated many U.S. housewives, flourished, with friends terming the pair inseparable. "She's a happy girl," commented a close associate. "She's successful and she's in love. What more does she need?"

"I'm happy she's found love with a wonderful man," was George Montgomery's reaction to the romance. "If Burt makes her happy, then I'm happy for her."

Miss Shore's former husband had recently received an offer from *Playgirl* magazine to follow Reynolds's lead and pose in the nude. He'd refused.

Burt guested on Dinah's show often and whenever her schedule allowed, she would visit him on his various movie locations – like *The Man Who Loved Cat Dancing* in Arizona's desert country in 1973.

Cat Dancing would have been a totally forgettable motion picture had it not been for a tragic incident that occurred on its Gila Bend location. David Whiting, a friend of actress Sarah Miles, Burt's co-star, killed himself. The press had a field day, and the town of Gila Bend seemed to revel in its brief notoriety.

According to testimony at the inquest, Miss Miles and Reynolds had enjoyed a drink together, after which she retired to her own motel room. There, she was confronted by a jealous and enraged Whiting, who savagely beat her. He fled, and Sarah called Burt for help. The actor rushed to his co-star's aid, spending the next few hours consoling her. Later that night, Whiting took his own life.

"It has happened in the past," Sarah explained to authorities, "and whenever he had hit me, he has always been so ashamed afterward, really remorseful."

Sordid minds suggested that the relationship between Reynolds and Miss Miles was something more than professional, but there was no real evidence to corroborate this. Indeed, few people working on the film gave these allegations serious consideration.

"The tragedy taught me who my friends are," said Burt. "First and foremost, there was Dinah. She was marvelous."

The romance didn't seem affected by what happened in Gila Bend. Dinah and Burt continued spending their free days together. With this man who was twenty years her junior, the singer even took up trail bike riding – taking a few spills in the process. "She's a classy lady," said Reynolds. "Her head's screwed on well, and she has great taste. That's why I'm not seeing other women. She's a great athlete, too. Kills me at tennis, but it's nice to go with a jock."

As was her nature, Dinah's description of the relationship was more romantic in tone: "It's a lovely world Burt and I have built together. We have something so great and we are so lucky. There really isn't a substitute for somebody."

***

"Dinah's Place," despite its shaky start, was doing well on NBC, airing on over two hundred stations. In May of 1974, the show even won an Emmy Award. Less than twenty four hours later, however, Miss Shore received a telegram from network vice-president Larry White, who congratulated her on the honor – then proceeded to inform her that her program had been cancelled.

The star's initial reaction to this stunning blow was to regard it as a prank. After all, how could NBC drop a show that was maintaining solid audience ratings with the commercially important group of women in the age range thirty to forty? It didn't make sense.

It was no joke. As explained by the network to Henry Jaffe, Dinah drew a very special audience that, unfortunately, did not stay tuned to NBC after her show ended. The programming executives rationalized that they needed an entry in her slot that would provide a stronger lead-in for the game shows airing later in the morning. Hence, "Dinah's Place" was axed.

The program was *not* cancelled by "mutual agreement," as NBC said in their press release regarding the action. As a high-ranking member of Dinah's staff said: "They, at least, owed her the courtesy of telling her in another way. I don't know where they got the idea that it was a *mutually agreeable* decision."

"Name That Tune" replaced "Dinah's Place," but that game show didn't last a year.

And, as for Miss Shore and company?

They hardly had time to catch their breath before a deal was negotiated for the lady to star on an all new ninety-minute variety-talk show, produced by her Winchester Productions. The entry would air over CBS owned-and-operated stations, as well as in syndication to other markets around the country. "Dinah!" as the new program would be tagged, was to debut in the Fall of 1974.

Staff for the new and longer project included Mr. Jaffe and Carolyn Raskin as executive producers; Fred Tatashore as producer; Glen Swanson to direct; and John Rodby serving as musical director. Tapings were to be done before a live audience at CBS Television City in Los Angeles.

With several successful talkers already on the air, Dinah and her people realized that if they were going to be successful in this new format, the show would have to be different. Just having celebrity guests come out and chat for a few minutes would not be enough, nor would the inclusion of a song or two score many points. The other shows did this sort of thing already – although their tunes were not being sung daily by the likes of Dinah Shore.

"We are a variety program as opposed to a talk show," explained a top member of the "Dinah!' production staff. "People don't come on our program and talk, then stand up and sing or tell jokes. Things are planned out carefully, and if somebody falls out at the last minute it can throw our whole theme off.

"When we do a production number – which is at least once a day – much time is spent on lighting and staging it properly. For instance, for a Chet Atkins guitar solo, we utilized photos of Picasso paintings as a backdrop. How many talk shows would go to that trouble?

"Also, a lot of pains go into our shows in booking guests who have something in common. For example, on a program that featured Joseph Wambaugh, the former policeman and author of books like *The Blue Knight*, we also booked Abe Vigoda, who plays 'Detective Fish' on television's 'Barney Miller.' On that same show, Richard Chamberlain read a speech from *Richard II* and Abe translated the Shakespearean dialogue into a form that 'Fish' would use.

"Often musical numbers Dinah sings on the show are determined by who her guests will be." When Richard Castellano came on, she did the love theme from *The Godfather*. Later, she and her guests continued the Sicilian idea by cooking spaghetti, which Castellano accidentally dropped on the front of his pin-striped suit.

One of the more memorable entries was a show that saluted Bing Crosby and featured, among others, Phil Harris and Pat Boone as guests. "We did several unusual things on that show," recalls the staffer. "First of all Pat Boone was actually a *surprise* guest. He came out dressed as Bing – with the hat and pipe – and did a good impersonation.

"We showed a clip from Crosby's first movie; Dinah and Bing danced together; and we also played the 'B' side to his hit records and he had to guess the 'A' half of the disc. He knew all but one and wound up singing fourteen tunes that day, instead of the two he'd been scheduled for.

"It was truly a warm, moving show. One of our best."

Like with Pat Boone and Bing, the "Dinah!" staff often tried to surprise a major guest star with somebody they were not expecting to see. When Andy Griffith appeared, former sidekick Don Knotts walked on; Ella Fitzgerald was caught off-guard by one of her staunchest admirers, Raymond Burr; and George Segal was served lunch on the air by waitress Lucille Ball.

"The main problem with mystery guests," said the staff member, "is keeping them hidden until it's time to go on."

"Entertainment" was the by-word on "Dinah!" which taped six shows (one for airing during vacations) in three days each week. Celebrity guests – many who refused to appear on other programs – came on the syndicated show, not to engage in in-depth conversation, but to have fun, whether light chatter, a relaxed song, a cooking session, or an impromptu stunt.

"Dinah does not want to embarrass anybody," her associate continued. "She tries to find out what a guest *doesn't* want to talk about so that she can avoid those areas. More than anything else, she is conscious of being a good hostess, a charming person, and treats the people who come on her show as if they were guests in her home."

Dinah had become an adept interviewer, ad-libbing most of her on-the-air conversations. She seldom knew who she'd be talking to on a particular day until she arrived at the studio. ("The exceptions are authors of new books: I *read* the book before I talk to the author!")

The undemanding atmosphere of her program notwithstanding, the star had, from time-to-time, come up with a few rather emotional conversations with her guests. "I once talked to Charo about her special relationship with Cugat," she reflected. "It was one of the most serious moments we've ever had on the show. On the other hand, Goldie Hawn informed me about what turned her on to certain men. 'I love a man's buns. Now take President Ford; I don't like his buns.'

"Shirley MacLaine talked about relationships between sexes. She says a man is a good lover if he can make you laugh after the passion."

Former escort Dick Martin had a great time whenever he appeared with Dinah: "I love to get outrageous and embarrass her on the air. I'll say, 'What happened to us, Dinah? Burt's a nice guy, but...' She just blusters."

Country-western artist Mel Tillis was another who had a great admiration for the hostess: "She understands country music better than other talk show moderators and is the easiest to work with. She's the only one who won't kid me about my stammering on the air. I think it's the motherly instinct in her."

Frequently, Dinah would invite the audience to ask questions of her guests. On one of those occasions when the celebrities included Debbie Reynolds, Hermoine Gingold, and Tillis, the query was: "Would you take your wife or husband to a nude beach?"

Recalled Mel: "When the question came 'round to me, I said, 'No. After twenty years of marriage, I have my wife believing that all men are created equal.'

"Well, it broke up the house. Dinah was so embarrassed that she blushed; Debbie couldn't stop laughing; and Hermoine fell over backwards."

When Ethel Waters guested on a segment, the audience requested that she sing "Dinah" – the tune she had made famous decades ago and which had served as inspiration for Miss Shore's professional name. The aging star of *Cabin in the Sky* delivered the song with some difficulty, but the deep affection she felt for her hostess was quite apparent, as was the love expressed to both these great performers through the audience's applause.

With its refreshing approach to a familiar format, "Dinah!" was a winner, capturing the bulk of the afternoon viewing audience in most areas that it aired. It was also a major recipient of Emmys, taking three of them for the 1975-76 season. (In 1974, the Hollywood Chapter of the Television Academy had also named the star "Woman of the Year.")

History was obviously repeating itself. No matter what aspect of show business she chose to venture into – with the exception of motion pictures – Dinah Shore always seemed to come up with the major honors, be it for records, radio, or the various television formats she mastered. Truly, her long list of awards would be difficult to match. No wonder Rosemary Clooney referred to her as "the champ."

***

Even with the show taping only three days a week, it was still an exhausting work schedule for Dinah. Yet the show didn't prevent her from taking on other professional activities. In 1975, for example, a new Dinah Shore album – for the Stanyan label – was on the market, in which she sang a selection of numbers by such contemporary composers as Michel Legrand, John Denver, and Burt Bacharach. Her own musical director, John Rodby, conducted the orchestra.

Television-wise, she not only went along with the idea to tape segments of her own show in such places as Las Vegas and Sydney, Australia, but also appeared on specials ("The Great American Celebration") and even served as hostess in 1976 for Carol Burnett's summer replacement series.

Entitled "Dinah and Her New Best Friends," the CBS Saturday night offering was actually a showcase for several talented newcomers: "Where can young people go these days?" Dinah said. "There's no Ed Sullivan, no 'Hollywood Palace.' Variety shows use stars. They can go on Johnny Carson and the other talk shows, but there's no time to properly produce a number and rehearse and mount it.

"So I told them I'd do Carol's show if I could take six wonderfully talented young people and give them a platform for eight weeks, a place to be seen."

The program was not too well received by critics. Writing in the *Los Angeles Times*, Cecil Smith called it "pretty feeble. Even Dinah, wearing some kind of blue Mother Hubbard that did nothing for her, seemed for once rather tired and ill at ease. Dinah is so effortless with her interviews and discussions on her daily show, yet she was stumbling and tongue-tied in talking with Jean Stapleton Saturday night."

Some show-business regulars thought it odd that Dinah would agree to do a prime time series, especially since she was already taping nine hours of afternoon fare each week. Why was she pushing herself so hard? She certainly didn't need the money or the prestige, since there were comparatively little of these incentives in the usually cheaply produced and sloppily planned network summer programming schedules. If she did want to help out a promising newcomer, she could always give him several bookings on her daytime series.

Perhaps this desire to keep overly busy was related more to her personal life. Maybe, as some wags theorized, it had something to do with the fact that her relationship with Burt Reynolds had cooled-off.

News of the break had become generally known as far back as April of 1975, while the actor was filming the disastrous Fox movie, *Lucky Lady*, in Mexico. Reports began filtering back to Tinseltown that Burt was telling cast and crew members that the romance was over. Adding fuel to the rumors was the knowledge that Dinah hadn't been down to visit Burt for several weeks.

"If we've split it's news to me," Dinah told the press, who were seeking a confirmation or denial of the stories. As with the two painful divorces she'd gone through, the lady believed in keeping her private life private, if possible.

The rumors continued to run rampant. Burt was having affairs with other women, the gossips said, including one with Lorna Luft.

"Burt and I liked each other very much at first," said the youngest daughter of the late Judy Garland. "We went together and had a lot of fun. I honestly feel that I didn't have anything to do with Burt's split with Dinah. I think he already had it in his mind. If I had not come along, it would have been somebody else."

Near the end of 1975, Dinah herself admitted publicly that her affair with Burt was over. Previously, she'd let her guard down once in an interview with a *Los Angeles Times* reporter when, in another context, she stated: "If there's one thing I've learned, it's that you don't trust men. They're adorable, but more for gamesmanship than trustsmanship."

She never went into the actual reasons for the split. Nobody really expected she would, since that would have been out of character. But later, when the truth of the situation had sunk in, she refused to go into mourning. "I'm going to do what I've always done," she announced, "and that is to work. I've found that is the best medicine for any ailment. I don't want people to feel

sorry for me. What's done is done, and we all have to go on. There's no sense in crying about yesterday – it's tomorrow that counts."

"I think she is indestructible," said her former pianist, Ticker Freeman. "Dinah's never going to get old. She's the only one of us who doesn't age."

11.

The Final Years

DINAH SHORE WAS NO WOMAN'S LIBBER. AND SHE DIDN'T CONSIDER herself to be chauvinistic in the slightest degree. "It's a man's world," she said. "A man shouldn't have to compete with a woman in his home and his office. We ask a man to go out and provide and be Big Daddy, and expect him to compete with a woman. He has a family to support. Suppose he loses his job to the woman? There are too many women today raising their children alone because the man couldn't provide. He couldn't meet the competition."

It's not that she advocated that the woman's place should be in the home. Such a position on her part would have been contradictory. Although she was the first to admit that all the important decisions in her stellar career had been made by men and that she'd enjoyed "leaning" on that gender, Dinah felt that when a woman did go into the business world – whether by choice of by circumstance – she was entitled to the same opportunities and pay as a man would receive. The unfortunate aspect, however, is that so many of these working girls insisted on considering the opposite sex as "the enemy."

More than once in her later years, Dinah herself had ventured outside the world of show business into what some might consider male territory. But in each instance, there seemed to be sufficient justification. In 1971, she was elected to the board of directors of the May Company Department Stores, an organization that did over one billion dollars in annual sales. According to the company's president, the appointment was made because of the star's "great sense of elegance and style, attributes of prime importance in our business..."

Dinah also agreed that her opinions could be quite valuable to the firm: "If they want to talk about shopping and stores and products, then I'm their girl."

Her real challenge to the masculine bureaucracy came outside the realm of business, and her victory resulted in the establishment of one of the richest women's golf tournaments in the country. At the time of Dinah's involvement, only thirteen men's events paid larger prizes to their winners.

As an unmarried woman who enjoyed playing golf, Dinah found it virtually impossible to join a Los Angeles country club. Tennis clubs were no problem, but when she tried to gain membership in one of the private male-oriented institutions that had a golf course, she was not welcome. It was nothing personal. Certainly her name on a membership roster would be quite prestigious, but it would be difficult to let *her* in and still bar other single girls.

"Apparently, the feeling is that a girl who isn't married is a potential home-wrecker," said Dinah.

She was in Florida during 1971 for the Colgate-Palmolive Company, sponsors of "Dinah's Place," and after entertaining and meeting with salesmen and executives of the firm, agreed to play a casual round of golf with company president David Foster. The group had such a fabulous time – betting twenty-five and fifty cents per hole – that they even played into a second day.

Foster noted that the executive wives had become interested in the game, following the players around like a gallery. He inquired if the singer might be interested in lending her name to a golf tournament for women. ("He said the girls weren't doing so well and they needed some encouragement. So I came home and started brushing up on my golf.")

In three short years, the Colgate-Dinah Shore Winners Circle Ladies Professional Golf Association Tournament (now called the Kraft Nabisco Championship), held each year at the Mission Hills Country Club in Palm Springs, grew from a $15,000-$30,000 event (as were the prizes at most ladies golf tournaments) to one that in 1985 awarded a total of $400,000 in prizes.

"Our first thought was to make women's golf on a par with men's as a spectator sport," says Dinah. "And we wanted equal pay for equal play. When Colgate lifted the purse to over $100,000, it stimulated interest in the rest of the ladies professional golf tours."

But the fact that her name was attached to a major golf tournament didn't immediately solve Dinah's problem with joining the elite country clubs. She was allowed to play on semi-private courses, but under what she called "unrealistic male rules," since the prime weekend starting times were reserved for men and the ladies couldn't tee off until the afternoon. "I'd be a whole lot better player if I could play regularly during the year," she said. "It's frustrating not to be allowed to play when you want."

Happily, Dinah was eventually accepted for membership at the prestigious Hillcrest Country Club. ("Now I don't have to sit around and wait until someone invites me to play.")

Possessing no ambitions to seriously rival champions like Sandra Palmer, Dinah was content to just "look good" when she played: "I have an intense desire to do whatever I do well, so as not to embarrass myself, but I don't have a terrific desire to win. I'm not sure I could do well under intensely competitive circumstances."

***

At age sixty-one, yet still tan, thin, and very attractive, Dinah Shore was continuously asked how she was able to remain in such good shape: "I try to get a lot of sleep – at least seven hours a night."

Formal diet, for the most part, was out for her. If she felt that she was gaining excess poundage, she simply ate less of everything. Working hard on her show and her daily tennis game were also effective means of weight control.

Maintaining a nice figure while hostessing a golf tournament was always a special problem, but Dinah had a little trick by which she could create such an illusion if the reality was uncooperative. As the star told *TV Guide* (1977), she had two daytime outfits at the tournament for each six rounds of play: "I wear only one each day, but I'm never sure before I wake up whether I'm going to need a fat outfit that day or a thin one. These things usually hinge on how much I have exercised the day before and how well I behaved at the table."

Sometimes she would appear on the course in an outfit a size too large: "It hangs on you. And a lot of people watching at home will say, 'Gosh, it looks like she's losing weight.'"

***

She dated Burt Reynolds occasionally after the passion had cooled, but, according to her intimates, that relationship had really totally ended. As one friend summed it up: "I think Dinah and Burt were very good for each other, but then a person's needs change." In the meantime, she saw others, such as sportscaster Frank Gifford and actors Wayne Rogers and Frank Langella.

Reynolds' commented on his former lady: "It's like breaking up with the American flag. Dinah was the great love of my life. But once you get past the fireworks stage, to pass on to the next stage gracefully, and then on to the next stage is really difficult."

With Missy and Jody living their own lives, Dinah resided alone – with her three dogs and ten Emmys – in a large one bedroom home, accented with high cathedral windows. Her life seemingly was a full one. The ever-popular talk-variety show, miscellaneous other professional activities, her annual golf tournament, tennis and, of course, her multitude of loving friends kept this marvelous entertainer's time well-filled and, as much as possible, her mind off any sorrow she might feel over not having really succeeded in any of her involvements with men. "I'm an individual person," she told *Good Housekeeping* in 1972, "and yet I think of my life as incomplete unless it's in terms of a man. So I guess my life hasn't been complete. It just never worked out that way. But I still believe that if a man and a woman can live in terms of each other, there is great strength in the relationship. That's what makes a marriage...To be truly in love with each other, a man and a woman have to be friends – and be able to share weaknesses as well as strengths...

"You build fantasies and you put people on pedestals and they put you on one. You endow them with those qualities you'd like them to have – and then both of you try to live up to the image. But the pictures you paint are one-dimensional, and it takes a long time to face up to reality. When you do, it hurts."

***

"I was frustrated, " Dinah said, explaining why she stopped doing her 90-minute daily talk show in 1980. "I am basically a singer, and I found out that I was doing a lot of talking but singing only two or three times a week, which wasn't enough. If you don't sing enough, you get out of the habit, like a cook who doesn't cook. So, now I'm just going to sing my little tonsils to the bone."

A few months after the show ended, she embarked on a 10-city concert tour, which included a four-day gig at Long Island's Westbury Music Fair.

There were also appearances on many television specials, including "The All-Time American Songbook" (1982), "Parade of Stars, " appearing as Helen Morgan (1983), All-Star Party for 'Dutch' Reagan" (1985), "America's Tribute to Bob Hope" (1988) and "Jack Benny: Comedy in Bloom" (1992).

Additionally, she was seen on some of TV's dramatic programs: "Hotel" (1987), "Murder She Wrote" (1989) and a 1979 CBS network movie, *Death Car on the Freeway*.

In January of 1985, Dinah was appointed to the board of directors of the MGM/UA Entertainment Company. "It's exciting for me," she said. "You have to do your homework....I believe there are only two other women in our business who have served on motion picture boards – Mary Pickford and Grace Kelly."

Four years later, at age 72, she was back on television., starring in "A Conversation with Dinah," a new half-hour interview show for The Nashville Network. "Television is what I am. It's who I am," she explained.

Perhaps her reason for returning to the tube was as a reaction to the Geraldos and Oprahs who were then hosting talk shows, which Dinah found "interesting". Actually, she was "absolutely fascinated" with topics those shows discussed, "because I thought those were things you only talked about in the doctor's office....It's not what I could do well."

The show, which was not taped in front of a studio audience, avoided confrontational issues that were the fodder of other talk programs. Said Dinah: "I want to get beneath the crusts of a lot of people who are wonderfully programmed and have built up a kind of wall between them (and everybody else), but I don't want to do it in a hurtful way....I sometimes think we are being talked to death on television. And, you don't hear much conversation.

"These won't be in-depth interviews; these will be 'in-shallow.' And if they turn out to be deep, I'm excited."

Among Dinah's early guests on the show were Nancy Reagan, Betty White, John Forsythe, Angie Dickinson, Rosemary Clooney, Jack Lemmon and Gerald Ford.

"Ours is an intimate portrait," Dinah said. "I don't want anybody to go away from the show and say, 'I wish I hadn't said that'."

"A Conversation with Dinah" was seen from 1989 to 1991.

***

Burt Reynolds: "I called Dinah and said I'd heard she was really ill. And she said, 'I'm great. I'm playing golf, and it's all fine. Don't come by.' And she passed away about a week or two later. She was the most amazing woman."

Dinah Shore died at her Beverly Hills home on February 24, 1994, just a few days short of her 78th birthday. Cause of death was ovarian cancer. Ex-husband George Montgomery and her two children were with her when she passed.

Half of her ashes are interred at Forest Lawn Memorial Park in Cathedral City (near Palm Springs, California). The other half are interred at Hillshide Memorial Park in Culver City, California.

***

Despite the personal pain she'd suffered throughout the years Dinah Shore carefully built herself into a cherished show-business institution. She swore that, had she the opportunity to start again, she wouldn't change her life's course one bit: "People grow from pain. They learn from the hurts they endure and, ultimately, gain a better understanding of both themselves and others."

Dinah traveled a long, difficult, albeit rewarding, road since she first departed Nashville to try her luck as a professional singer in the "big time." She may not have accomplished every personal goal, or found the all-encompassing happiness that she'd always yearned for. Few people do. Nevertheless, it was a remarkable journey.

Bibliography

(Partial List)

Crichton, K.; "Pride of the Clan"; *Colliers*, July 25, 1942.

"Dynamic Dinah"; *Time*, October 19, 1942.

Beatty, Jerome; "Hot Whispers"; *American Magazine*, April, 1943.

Jefferson, Sally; "Gay Romance"; *Photoplay*, September, 1943.

"Dinah for Shore"; *Newsweek*, October 16, 1944.

Arnold, Maxine; "They'll Be Seeing You"; *Movieland*, January, 1945.

"Is There Anything Finer?"; *Newsweek*, June 30, 1947.

Johnson, Grady; "The Dinah Shore Story"; *Coronet*, November, 1952.

"Dinah's Showcaser"; *Newsweek*, December 8, 1952.

Lindsay, C. H. ; "She's Still Winning Her Fight for Happiness"; *Woman's Home Companion*, February, 1953.

"Dinah, Is There Anyone Finer?"; *TV Guide*, June 26, 1953.

Wilson, Liza; "Why Dinah Goes Home"; *American Weekly*, October 11, 1953.

"An Artist Off Stage, Too"; *TV Guide*, November 27, 1953.

"Dinah's Magic Touch"; *TV Guide*, December 7, 1957.

"Is There Anyone Finah?"; *Time*, December 16, 1957.

Ardmore, Jane; "You Get Love By Giving Love"; *Family Circle*, January, 1958.

Reed, Dena; "Who Says Star Marriages Can't Work?"; *Movieland*, July, 1958.

Baskett, K.; "I Had to Be Loved"; *Redbook*, October 1958.

Oppenheimer, Peer J.; "First Lady of Television"; *Family Weekly*, October 5, 1958.

Whitney, Dwight; "Dinah is an Exception"; *TV Guide*, April 18, 1959.

Hurst, Tricia; "Nobody Loved Me"; *Photoplay*, July, 1959.

Martin, Pete; "I Call on Dinah Shore"; *Saturday Evening Post*, October 19, 1959.

Hubler, R.G.; "The Indestructable Dinah"; *Coronet*, November, 1959.

Tornabene, Lyn; "Miss Shore's TV Wardrobe"; *Cosmopolitan*, November, 1959.

"Dual Lives of Dinah"; *Life*, February 1, 1960.

Johnson, Arlene; "I Hope My Daughter Missy Makes the Same Mistake I Did"; *Photoplay*, April, 1960.

Schroeder, Carl; "How a 'Good Wife' Failed"; *Good Housekeeping*, April, 1962.

Jenkins, Dan; "No Longer a Prisoner of Perfection"; *TV Guide*, April 20, 1963.

Oppenheimer, Peer J.; "Why I'm Quitting"; *Family Weekly*, May 26, 1963.

Hano, Arnold; "She's Working with a New Recipe"; *TV Guide*, March 6, 1971.

Bell, Joseph N.; "Dinah Shore"; *Good Housekeeping*, August, 1972.

Higham, Charles; "Nothin' Could Be Finah for Dinah Shore"; *New York Times*, August 27, 1972.

Ardmore, Jane; "Our Love is Here to Stay..."; *Photoplay*, June, 1973.

St. John, Michael; "Burt Walked Out On Me"; *TV Radio Talk*, November, 1975.

Facter, Sue; "Dinah Shore"; *Celebrity*, September, 1976.

Handley, Alan; "A Kiss for Dinah"; *TV Guide*, January 15, 1977.

Durslag, Melvin; "Still in Fashion: Small Purses"; *TV Guide*, April 2, 1977.

Klemesrud, Judy; "Dinah, Ageless, Is Reveling in Her 60's"; *New York Times*, April 26, 1981.

Hawn, Jack; "The Golfing Life: Folksy Dinah Shore: She's Out of Doors and Involved"; *Los Angeles Times*, March 31, 1985.

The Films of Dinah Shore

1. *Thank Your Lucky Stars*; Warner Brothers (1943); *Director*: David Butler. *Cast*: Humphrey Bogart; Eddie Cantor, Jack Carson, Bette Davis, Errol Flynn, John Garfield, Olivia de Havilland, Joan Leslie, Ida Lupino, Dennis Morgan, Ann Sheridan, Dinah Shore, Alexis Smith.

2. *Up in Arms*; Samuel Goldwyn (1944); Color; *Director*: Elliott Nugent. *Cast*: Danny Kaye, Dinah Shore, Dana Andrews, Constance Dowling, Louis Calhern, Lyle Talbot, Margaret Dumont.

3. *Follow the Boys*; Universal (1944); *Director*: Edward Sutherland. *Cast*: Marlene Dietrich, George Raft, Verna Zorina, Dinah Shore, W.C. Fields, Jeanette MacDonald, Maria Montez, The Andrews Sisters, Sophie Tucker, Nigel Bruce, Gale Sondergaard.

4. *Belle of the Yukon*; RKO (1944); Color; *Director*: William Seiter. *Cast*: Randolph Scott, Gypsy Rose Lee, Dinah Shore, Charles Winninger, William Marshall, Florence Bates.

5. *Till the Clouds Roll By*; MGM (1946); Color; *Director*: Richard Whorf. *Musical Sequences Staged By*: Robert Alton, Vincente Minnelli. Cast: June Allyson, Lucille Bremer, Judy Garland, Kathryn Grayson, Van Heflin, Lena Horne, Van Johnson, Angela Lansbury, Tony Martin, Dinah Shore, Frank Sinatra, Robert Walker.

6. *Make Mine Music*; Disney (1946); Color; *Directors*: Jack Kinney, Clyde Geronimi, Hamilton Luske, Robert Cormack, Joshua Meador. *Voices*: Nelson Eddy, Dinah Shore, Benny Goodman and Orchestra, The Andrews Sisters, Jerry Colonna, Andy Russell, Sterling Holloway, The Pied Pipers, The King's Men, The Ken Darby Chorus.

7. *Fun and Fancy Free*; Disney (1947); Color; *Live-action Director*: William Morgan. *Cartoon Directors*: Jack Kinney, Bill Roberts, Hamilton Luske. *Cast*: Edgar Bergen, Dinah Shore (voice only), Luana Patten, Charlie McCarthy, Mortimer Snerd. *Cartoon Voices*: Anita Gordon, Cliff Edwards, Billy Gilbert, Clarence Nash, The King's Men, The Dinning Sisters, The Starlighters.

8. *Aaron Slick from Punkin Crick*; Paramount (1952); Color; *Director*: Claude Binyon. *Cast*: Alan Young, Dinah Shore, Robert Merrill, Adele Jergens, Veda Ann Borg.

9. *Oh, God!*; Warner Brothers (1977); Color; Director: Carl Reiner. Cast: George Burns, John Denver, Teri Garr, Donald Pleasance, Ralph Bellamy, Paul Sorvino, Barry Sullivan, Dinah Shore (*cameo*).

10. *HealtH*; 20th Century-Fox (1980); Color; Director: Robert Altman. Cast: Carol Burnett, Glenda Jackson, James Garner, Lauren Bacall, Paul Dooley, Alfre Woodard, Donald Moffat, Henry Gibson, Dinah Shore (*cameo*).

The Best-Selling Records of Dinah Shore

(According to *Billboard*)

Bluebird
1941
"Yes, My Darling Daughter"
"I Hear a Rhapsody"
" 'Jim'"
1942
"Blues in the Night"
"Miss You"

Victor
1942
"One Dozen Roses"
"Dearly Beloved"

1943
"Why Don't You Fall in Love With Me?"
"You'd Be So Nice to Come Home To"
" 'Murder,' He Says"
1944
"I'll Walk Alone"
1945
"Candy"
"Along the Navajo Trail"

Columbia
1946
"Shoo-Fly Pie"
"Laughing on the Outside"
"The Gypsy"
"Doin' What Comes Natur'lly"
1947
"For Sentimental Reasons"
"Anniversary Song"
"I Wish I Didn't Love You So"
"You Do"
"How Soon"
1948
"Little White Lies"
"Buttons and Bows"
"Lavender Blue"
1949
"Far Away Places"
"So in Love"
"Baby, It's Cold Outside"
"A Wonderful Guy"
"Dear Hearts and Gentle People"
1950
"It's So Nice to Have a Man Around the House"

RCA Victor

1950

"My Heart Cries for You"

1951

"A Penny a Kiss" (with Tony Martin)

"In Your Arms" (with Tony Martin)

"Sweet Violets"

1952

"Blues in Advance"

1955

"Whatever Lola Wants"

"Love and Marriage"

1956

"Stolen Love"

"I Could Have Danced All Night"

1957

"Chantez-Chantez"

"The Cattle Call"

"Fascination"

Index

*Numbers in **bold** indicate photographs*

About the Author

Michael B. Druxman is a veteran Hollywood screenwriter whose credits include *Cheyenne Warrior* with Kelly Preston; *Dillinger and Capone* starring Martin Sheen and F. Murray Abraham; and *The Doorway* with Roy Scheider, which he also directed.

He is also a prolific playwright, his one-person play, *Jolson*, having had numerous productions around the country. Other produced stage credits include one-person plays about Clark Gable, Carole Lombard, Spencer Tracy and Orson Welles. These and plays about Errol Flynn, Clara Bow, Maurice Chevalier, Jeanette MacDonald and Nelson Eddy and Basil Rathbone have been individually published under the collective title of *The Hollywood Legends*.

Additionally, Mr. Druxman is the author of many other published books, including several nonfiction works about Hollywood, its movies, and the people who make them (e.g., *Basil Rathbone: His Life and His Films, Make It Again, Sam: A Survey of Movie Remakes, One Good Film Deserves Another: A Survey of Movie Sequels, Merv* [Griffin] and *The Musical: From Broadway to Hollywood*).

He has written three novels, *Nobody Drowns in Mineral Lake, Shadow Watcher* and *Murder in Babylon*, a book of short stories, entitled *Dracula Meets Jack the Ripper & Other Revisionist Histories*, plus the humorous revisionist history, *Once Upon a Time in Hollywood: From the Secret Files of Harry Pennypacker*, and *Family Secret*, a non-fiction book co-authored with Warren Hull, which reveals the true facts behind the 1947 murder of mobster "Bugsy" Siegel in Beverly Hills.

An acknowledged Hollywood historian, he has also written television documentaries and has been interviewed for various retrospective featurettes that have accompanied DVD releases of classic films (e.g. *The Maltese Falcon*, etc.).

Mr. Druxman is a former Hollywood publicist of 35 years experience who has represented many film and television stars, as well as noted directors, producers and composers. One of his Academy Award campaigns is often mentioned in books dealing with Oscar's history.

He has taught various dramatic writing and film appreciation courses in an adult university and is the author of *How to Write a Story...Any Story: The Art of Storytelling*, which has been used as a text in several colleges. He is often invited to speak to groups of aspiring film and television professionals to discuss screenwriting and the realities of show business.

A native of Seattle, who graduated from Garfield High School and the University of Washington, Mr. Druxman moved with his wife, Sandy, from Los Angeles to Austin, TX in 2009.

His two memoirs, *My Forty-Five Years in Hollywood and How I Escaped Alive* and *Life, Liberty & The Pursuit of Hollywood* are published by Bear Manor Media.

CPSIA information can be obtained at www.ICGtesting.com
Printed in the USA
BVOW06*1830140815

412946BV00007B/157/P